TEACHING CHILDREN FITNESS

Becoming a Master Teacher

THOMAS RATLIFFE, EdD
Florida State University

LARAINE McCRAVEY RATLIFFE, MAT
Florida State University School

Human Kinetics

Library of Congress Cataloging-in-Publication Data

Ratliffe, Thomas, 1947-
    Teaching children fitness : becoming a master teacher / Thomas
Ratliffe, Laraine McCravey Ratliffe.
      p.   cm.
    ISBN 0-87322-478-7
    1. Physical fitness for children--Study and teaching.
I. Ratliffe, Laraine McCravey, 1946-   II. Title.
GV443.R28   1994
613.7'042--dc20   93-42449
                                        CIP

ISBN: 0-87322-478-7

Copyright © 1994 by Human Kinetics Publishers, Inc.

Acquisitions Editor: Scott Wikgren
Series Editor: George Graham, PhD
AMTP Content Editor: Christine Hopple
Developmental Editor: Julia Anderson
Assistant Editors: Ed Giles, Lisa Sotirelis, Matt Scholz, Dawn Roselund
Copyeditor: Ginger Rodriguez
Proofreader: Anne Byler
Production Director: Ernie Noa
Typesetting and Text Layout: Sandra Meier
Illustration Coordinators: Tara Welsch, Kris Slamans
Text Designer: Keith Blomberg
Cover Designer: Jody Boles
Photographer (cover): Bob Veltri
Interior Art: Mary Yemma Long, Gretchen Walters, Kathy Boudreau-Fuoss
Cover Models: Andrew Baffi, Nick Baffi, Emily Carstenson, Jennifer Shephard
Printer: United Graphics

Printed in the United States of America

10 9 8 7 6 5 4 3 2 1

Human Kinetics
P.O. Box 5076, Champaign, IL 61825-5076
1-800-747-4457

Canada: Human Kinetics, Box 24040, Windsor, ON N8Y 4Y9
1-800-465-7301 (in Canada only)

Europe: Human Kinetics, P.O. Box IW14, Leeds LS16 6TR, England
0532-781708

Australia: Human Kinetics, P.O. Box 80, Kingswood 5062, South Australia
618-374-0433

New Zealand: Human Kinetics, P.O. Box 105-231, Auckland 1
(09) 309-2259

Contents

Series Preface

In the United States most children spend 6 to 7 years in elementary schools, from kindergarten through sixth grade. Assume that they participate in instructional physical education classes twice a week for the entire time. Each class is 30 minutes long—a total of 36 hours a year and 216 hours over 6 years. Because of interruptions such as snow days, field trips, school plays, absences, and arriving late to physical education class, the time actually spent in physical education may be closer to 150 hours—perhaps less. Still 150 hours is a substantial amount of time. But what do children learn in that time? What is realistic to expect they might learn?

The answers vary. Some children might learn that physical activity is enjoyable, something they choose to do on their own with friends after school and on weekends. Others might learn that they are not good at sports and search for other ways to spend their leisure time. Others might really like their PE classes and the teacher but, given a choice, prefer to watch television or sit around when they're at home. The 150 hours, hopefully more, that a child spends in physical education classes influence his or her decisions—as a child, and for a lifetime!

What do we expect children to learn in elementary school physical education? Until recently the answer to this question was left solely to the individual teacher or school district. Physical educators across the United States had no universal sense of the outcomes that might accrue from quality programs of physical education. But this changed in 1992, when the National Association for Sport and Physical Education (NASPE) completed 7 years of work on a document titled *The Physically Educated Person.* This document outlined, for the first time, a nationally developed and endorsed framework for planning and evaluating physical education programs, from preschool through Grade 12 (Franck et al., 1991). This book, and the other volumes in this series, were developed using the outcomes and benchmarks developed by NASPE as a general guide.

As you might imagine, the American Master Teacher Program (AMTP) struggled with how to organize the content. Should there be one book? Several books? Which model should we use to organize the content? Ultimately we chose to develop five books on the following topics: basic movement skills and concepts, games, gymnastics, dance, and fitness concepts. We decided to publish several books instead of just one because it seemed to be the most widely understood approach to organizing the content in physical education. It also provided the opportunity to involve several authors who were recognized for their expertise in their respective areas.

As we were considering possible authors, we made lists of who we thought were the best qualified individuals to write these books. In each instance, we are delighted to say, the author or authors we thought most qualified accepted our invitation to write the book. The books are as follows:

- *Teaching Children Movement Concepts and Skills: Becoming a Master Teacher* by Craig Buschner
- *Teaching Children Dance: Becoming a Master Teacher* by Theresa Purcell
- *Teaching Children Gymnastics: Becoming a Master Teacher* by Peter Werner
- *Teaching Children Games: Becoming a Master Teacher* by David Belka
- *Teaching Children Fitness: Becoming a Master Teacher* by Tom and Laraine Ratliffe

In addition, we want to thank Dr. Paula Ely, principal of Margaret Beeks Elementary School in Blacksburg, VA, for her ongoing support of various aspects of the American Master Teacher Program.

Each book is divided into two parts. The first part contains five chapters, which include a description of the content, an explanation of how it is organized, and most importantly the reasons why the author or authors believe that content is important for children to learn. One problem that has plagued physical education in elementary schools is that programs all too often have lacked an underlying theory or purpose. It seemed that teachers were just trying to entertain the children rather than to actually teach them. For this reason, we hope you will begin reading this book by carefully reading Part I so that you can better understand the content—and *why* it is important for children to learn.

Part II contains the activities, or learning experiences (LEs). Five chapters contain the actual "stuff" to do with children. It is more than just stuff, however. Part II presents a logical progression of activities designed to lead children toward a heightened understanding and improved competence in the content described in the book. After you read the content described in Part I, you will be better able to envision where the LEs are leading—and the importance of the progression and sequencing of these activities will be clear to you. From the standpoint of the author, and ultimately the children, it would be unfortunate if a teacher completely skipped Part I and then searched Part II for activities that appeared to be the most fun and exciting—and then taught them in a haphazard way without any logical sequencing or order to the program. Children truly enjoy learning! These books are designed to help them do just that; the purpose is not just to keep them busy for a few minutes several times a week.

Finally, it is important to emphasize that *the contents of all five books are important* for the children's physical education. One danger in doing a series of books is that a mistaken impression might be given that a content area can be skipped altogether. This is not the case. Just as it wouldn't make sense for math teachers to skip subtraction or division because they didn't like to "take things away" or "weren't very good at it," it doesn't make sense to skip dance or gymnastics, for example, because a teacher has never had a course in it or isn't confident about teaching it. We realize, however, that many physical education teachers feel less confident about teaching dance or gymnastics; this is the primary reason the books were written—and why the AMTP was founded. It is certainly OK to feel anxious or unconfident about teaching one, or more, of the content areas. It's not OK, however, not to teach them because of these feelings. Many of us have experienced these same feelings, but with experience, work, and support, we have gradually incorporated them into our programs—and done so in ways that are both beneficial and enjoyable for children. This is what we want to help you to do as well. And that's why the books were written and the AMTP was developed.

Each of the five content books also has a companion videotape that provides examples of actual lessons selected from the learning experiences. These consolidated lessons show you how a few LEs might be developed with children. In addition to the videotape, workshops are available through the American Master Teacher Program to help you gain a better understanding of the content and how it is taught. The authors of the books realize that making the transition from a traditional program to teaching this content is not easy, and yet increasingly teachers are realizing that children deserve more than simply being entertained in the name of physical education. We hope you will find the books worthwhile—and helpful—and that the children you teach will benefit!

George Graham
Cofounder and Director of Curriculum
     and Instruction
American Master Teacher Program

Preface

"You have been given a wonderful gift—a healthy body. Why not take excellent care of it and always keep your body in the best possible condition so it can serve you well?"

A sixth-grade physical education teacher gave this message to one of the authors, and it made a lasting impression. Good health, an active lifestyle, and a high level of physical fitness form the foundation of our lives. As teachers, we would like to pass this message on to future generations of children.

Our approach to teaching fitness is based on developing a cognitive understanding of fitness concepts through practical, hands-on experiences. Just talking about fitness or just doing fitness exercises is not enough, but together explaining and doing can make a difference.

We became interested in teaching fitness concepts during the mid-1970s while working as laboratory assistants for Russ Pate's exercise physiology classes at the University of South Carolina. Later, as elementary physical education teachers, we began to adapt exercise physiology concepts so children could understand the information. We were excited to find that an old educational theory worked—you can teach almost anything to anybody by breaking down the information into small enough parts to match the learner's cognitive development.

In 1979, at the national convention of the American Alliance for Health, Physical Education, Recreation and Dance (AAHPERD) in New Orleans, we presented our ideas about teaching fitness. We have been teaching fitness concepts to children ever since, adopting and adapting ideas from teachers and writers, and we welcome the opportunity to share our experiences in this book.

Teaching Children Fitness: Becoming a Master Teacher is one of a series of content-related books that comprise the American Master Teacher Program. This book is written for both beginning and experienced elementary physical education teachers who want to educate their students about fitness. Numerous fitness games and activity books for children are available, and numerous textbooks exist for high school students and adults. Unlike some of those texts, this book is not just a collection of fitness games and activities. We have designed this book to help elementary physical education teachers identify relevant fitness information, organize the fitness curriculum into a logical sequence, and provide learning experiences to help children accomplish specific fitness objectives. We have broken down complex fitness information into simple concepts that relate to children's needs, interests, and cognitive development. *Teaching Children Fitness: Becoming a Master Teacher* will provide you with instructional strategies to teach your elementary children about fitness concepts by using enjoyable learning experiences that combine cognitive instruction with physical activities.

Our major goal is to educate children about physical fitness through active, hands-on learning experiences, not to train children into shape. Due to the vast content of physical education (Belka, 1994; Buschner, 1994; Purcell, 1994; Werner, 1994) and the limited amount of class time, it is not realistic to expect children to become physically fit just by attending physical education classes. Developing highly fit children and producing high scores on fitness tests are desirable outcomes, but not realistic objectives of a school-based physical education program. Learning fitness concepts, experiencing appropriate fitness activities, and stimulating children to participate in fitness opportunities outside of class time are realistic goals.

Teaching Children Fitness is divided into two parts. Part I (chapters 1 to 5) provides background information about children's fitness, variables that can affect teaching situations, an overview of the curriculum content, principles to follow when teaching fitness, and ideas for assessing children's progress in fitness. Part II (chapters 6 to 10) provides a sample of school-tested learning experiences organized into five different categories to help children learn important fitness concepts. A reference list, suggested readings, and additional resources appear at the end of the book.

Participation in and enjoyment of physical activity is one of life's finest gifts that every youngster should have an opportunity to experience. As educators, we can make this happen.

We are grateful to the many people we have worked with over the years who have helped us develop our ideas for teaching fitness. Our interest in exercise physiology was stimulated by Russ Pate, who encouraged us to teach fitness concepts to children. Our approach and methods of teaching children have been greatly influenced by Jane Young and George Graham. We've enjoyed their friendship and benefited from their eagerness to share their knowledge and experiences with us.

We have had an opportunity to work with many wonderful teachers and children over the years and would like to recognize the schools in South Carolina, Georgia, Massachusetts, and Florida that have stimulated ideas for this book—Congaree, Pine Ridge, Hollsenbeck, Winterville, Marks Meadow, Florence, Leeds, and the Florida State University School. Thanks to Scott Wikgren and the people at Human Kinetics Publishers for supporting children's physical education. And thanks to George Graham, Christine Hopple, and Julia Anderson for providing guidance and editing to make this book possible.

Developmentally Appropriate Fitness

In 1992 the National Association for Sport and Physical Education (NASPE) published a document entitled *Developmentally Appropriate Physical Education Practices for Children*. The document, developed by the executive committee of the Council on Physical Education for Children (COPEC), represents the collective wisdom of many physical educators about what good elementary physical education is. The principles NASPE espoused in the document guided the development of this and the other four books in this series.

Part I begins with an overview of developmentally appropriate fitness, why it should be part of a quality elementary PE program, and how this approach differs from what has been traditionally taught in physical education. Chapter 1 also includes a definition of the physically educated person, including psychomotor, cognitive, and affective objectives, and a discussion of the significance of this definition for children's fitness instruction.

Virtually no two teaching situations are identical in physical education. Chapter 2 provides several suggestions on how you can structure your program to fit the idiosyncrasies of your school. This chapter includes ideas for teaching lessons with limited space, equipment, and time. As explained in this chapter, quality programs can be developed in less-than-ideal situations, but it's not easy.

A complete description of the content, including definitions of terms specific to the content area, is provided in chapter 3. As you review the content of all five books, you will quickly see that they contain much more than fun games and activities that are designed simply to keep children occupied for 30 minutes or so. Each content area outlines a developmentally appropriate curriculum designed to provide children with a logical progression of tasks leading to skillfulness in, and enjoyment of, physical activity.

Chapter 4 describes and discusses the key teaching principles that are used to provide developmentally appropriate experiences for children. This chapter applies pedagogical principles as they relate specifically to teaching the content included in the book. As you know, each of the five content areas has unique characteristics that master teachers are aware of as they teach their lessons.

The final chapter in Part I is on assessment. It describes practical ways to assess how well children are learning the concepts and skills related to the content being taught. As we enter the 21st century, educators are increasingly being required to document, in realistic ways, the progress their children are making. This requirement presents unique challenges to the elementary school physical educators who may teach 600 or more children each week. Chapter 5 provides some realistic suggestions for ways to formatively assess what children are learning.

Chapter 1

Why Is It Important to Teach Children Fitness?

Physical education has many possible purposes, ranging from the development of motor skills like throwing and catching to learning the training principles of exercise to the development of social skills like cooperation. A desired outcome of all these purposes is to help children grow up to be physically active adults.

The content area of physical fitness includes the learning experiences associated with achieving optimal health in the components of cardiorespiratory endurance, muscular strength and endurance, flexibility, and body composition. The approach we take reflects our belief that teaching fitness should help students learn cognitive information about physical fitness concepts, involve them in learning experiences that help them apply fitness information, and lead them to value an active, fitness-oriented lifestyle (see Figure 1.1).

You won't see fitness scores as a specific objective in this book. Fitness scores should not be the only criteria used to evaluate the effectiveness of a physical education program, just as test scores should not be the only criteria to evaluate the effectiveness of a math or reading program. Making progress on fitness assessments, learning to do skills and exercises properly, learning fitness concepts, and developing positive attitudes about physical activity may be more important for students than scoring high on fitness tests.

Your teaching of fitness should complement your teaching of motor skills, movement concepts, dance, gymnastics, and games to help children develop into physically educated people. The National Association for Sport and Physical Education has provided a definition of the physically educated person (Franck et al., 1991), shown in Figure 1.2.

All the American Master Teacher Program books are designed to help you achieve these outcomes with your students (Belka, 1994; Buschner, 1994; Purcell, 1994; Werner, 1994). This fifth book in the set is designed to help you teach physical fitness to children. In this first chapter we'll define fitness; briefly describe the evolution of fitness in the physical education curriculum; explain the relationship between physical fitness scores, physical activity habits, and health; provide a picture of the present status of children's fitness; list the beneficial outcomes for fit children; and explain our approach for how to best teach fitness to children in school physical education programs.

What Is Fitness?

Until recently, physical fitness was defined as the capacity to carry out daily tasks without undue fatigue and with ample energy to enjoy leisure pursuits and to meet unforeseen emergencies. This definition was fine when daily tasks required vigorous effort and leisure time meant more than watching TV. For today's living, a more appropriate definition of fitness is the capacity of the heart, blood vessels,

Figure 1.1   Developing an active lifestyle.

lungs, and muscles to function at optimum efficiency (Pate, 1983). Fitness is a physical state of well-being that allows people to perform daily activities with vigor, reduce their risk of health problems related to lack of exercise, and establish a base of fitness for participation in a variety of physical activities.

Physical fitness includes both health-related and skill-related components. Health-related fitness components—cardiorespiratory efficiency, muscular strength and endurance, flexibility, and body composition—focus on factors that promote optimum health and prevent the onset of diseases and problems associated with inactivity. Skill-related components focus on abilities and skills associated with performance in movement, sports, dance, and gymnastics. These skill-related components, highly influenced by heredity, include agility, balance, coordination, power, and speed. The emphasis of this book is the health-related fitness components. The skill-related components are addressed in the other American Master Teacher Program content books (Belka, 1994; Buschner, 1994; Purcell, 1994; Werner, 1994).

The Evolution of Fitness in Physical Education

Physical fitness has always been a part of physical education, but the emphasis has been on doing fitness activities and getting in shape rather than on the educational aspects of why and how. In the

years before and after World Wars I and II, physical education was viewed as an opportunity to physically train the youth of America. Then in the 1950s, the Kraus-Weber studies showing American children falling behind European children in fitness levels (Kraus & Hirschland, 1954) produced a renewed emphasis on fitness. Again, the emphasis was on getting children fit through exercise programs in schools.

Prior to 1980, the majority of physical education programs primarily evaluated skill-related components of fitness including speed, agility, and power. Typical tests included the 50-yard dash, shuttle run, and softball throw. In 1968 Dr. Kenneth Cooper's first book, *Aerobics*, helped the American public understand the importance of cardiorespiratory fitness and challenged them to counter the epidemics of heart disease, obesity, and other health-related problems. This redefinition of physical fitness in terms of health rather than skill performance resulted in the American Alliance for Health, Physical Education, Recreation and Dance (AAHPERD) publication of the Health Related Fitness Test in 1980. This test used a distance run, sit-ups, skinfold measurements, and a sit-and-reach measurement to assess the health-related components of cardiorespiratory endurance, muscular strength and endurance, body composition, and flexibility. Subsequently, in 1989 AAHPERD published the Physical Best Educational Kit to promote fitness education in the schools. In recent years, the focus of teaching fitness has branched out to touch all the ingredients of human wellness

A Physically Educated Person

- **Has** learned skills necessary to perform a variety of physical activities:
    1. Moves using concepts of body awareness, space awareness, effort, and relationships
    2. Demonstrates competence in a variety of manipulative, locomotor, and nonlocomotor skills
    3. Demonstrates competence in combinations of manipulative, locomotor, and nonlocomotor skills performed individually and with others
    4. Demonstrates competence in many different forms of physical activity
    5. Demonstrates proficiency in a few forms of physical activity
    6. Has learned how to learn new skills

- **Is** physically fit:
    7. Assesses, achieves, and maintains physical fitness
    8. Designs safe, personal fitness programs in accordance with principles of training and conditioning

- **Does** participate regularly in physical activity:
    9. Participates in health-enhancing physical activity at least three times a week
    10. Selects and regularly participates in lifetime physical activities

- **Knows** the implications of and the benefits from involvement in physical activities:
    11. Identifies the benefits, costs, and obligations associated with regular participation in physical activity
    12. Recognizes the risk and safety factors associated with regular participation in physical activity
    13. Applies concepts and principles to the development of motor skills
    14. Understands that wellness involves more than being physically fit
    15. Knows the rules, strategies, and appropriate behaviors for selected physical activities
    16. Recognizes that participation in physical activity can lead to multicultural and international understanding
    17. Understands that physical activity provides the opportunity for enjoyment, self-expression, and communication

- **Values** physical activity and its contributions to a healthful lifestyle:
    18. Appreciates the relationships with others that result from participation in physical activity
    19. Respects the role that regular physical activity plays in the pursuit of lifelong health and well-being
    20. Cherishes the feelings that result from regular participation in physical activity

---

Figure 1.2   Outcomes of quality physical education programs. *Note.* The "Physically Educated Person" document containing these outcomes and accompanying benchmarks (see Figure 1.5) is available from NASPE at 1900 Association Drive, Reston, VA 22091-1599, 1-800-321-0789.

From *Physical Education Outcomes: A Project of the National Association for Sport and Physical Education* by M. Franck, G. Graham, H. Lawson, T. Loughrey, R. Ritson, M. Sanborn, and V. Seefeldt (The Outcomes Committee of NASPE), 1991. Reprinted by permission of the National Association for Sport and Physical Education, Reston, VA.

including regular vigorous exercise, diet, elimination of smoking, dealing with stress, and responsible use of alcohol and drugs.

The Relationship Between Physical Activity, Physical Fitness, and Health

Teaching fitness has the potential to influence children in all the health-related and wellness components identified by AAHPERD. The contributions of physical activity to a healthier and happier life are well documented (Seefeldt, 1986). Table 1.1 lists some of the physical and mental health benefits of regular physical activity (Corbin & Lindsey, 1991).

People can only fulfill their potential when their bodies are healthy and fit. Unfortunately, many people in our society are not healthy and are not getting sufficient activity to be physically fit (Ross & Pate, 1987).

In the past, the normal routine of daily living required vigorous work and activity. Children did more walking for transportation and played outside more often. Today, concerns about safety prevent many parents from even letting their kids play in

Table 1.1   Physical and Mental Health Benefits of Proper Exercise

Major physical benefit	Related benefits	Major mental health benefit	Related benefits
Improved cardiovascular fitness	• Stronger heart muscle • Lower heart rate • Possible reduction in blood pressure • Reduced blood fat, including low density lipids (LDL) • Possible resistance to atherosclerosis • Possible improved peripheral circulation • Improved coronary circulation • Resistance to "emotional storm" • Less chance of heart attack • Greater chance of surviving a heart attack • Increased protective high density lipids (HDL) • Increased oxygen carrying capacity of the blood	Reduction in mental tension	• Relief of depression • Improved sleep habits • Fewer stress symptoms • Ability to enjoy leisure • Possible work improvement
Greater lean body mass and less body fat	• Greater work efficiency • Less susceptibility to disease • Improved appearance • Less incidence of self-concept problems related to obesity	Opportunity for social interactions	• Improved quality of life
Improved strength and muscular endurance	• Greater work efficiency • Less chance of muscle injury • Decreased chance of low back problems • Improved performance in sports • Improved ability to meet emergencies	Resistance to fatigue	• Ability to enjoy leisure • Improved quality of life • Improved ability to meet some stressors
Improved flexibility	• Greater work efficiency • Less chance of muscle injury • Less chance of joint injury • Decreased chance of low back problems • Improved sports performance	Opportunity for successful experience	• Improved self-concept • Opportunity to recognize and accept personal limitations
Other health benefits of exercise and physical activity	• Extended life • Quicker recovery after hard work • Decreased chance of adult-onset diabetes • Less chance of osteoporosis • Reduced risk of certain cancers	Improved physical fitness	• Improved sense of well-being • Improved self-concept • Improved appearance

Note. From Charles B. Corbin and Ruth Lindsey, *Concepts of Physical Fitness with Laboratories,* copyright © 1991 Wm. C. Brown Communications, Inc., Dubuque, Iowa. All rights reserved. Adapted by permission.

the neighborhoods. When both parents are working, they are not able to transport their kids to recreational opportunities and are not home to spend time playing with their children.

Modern machines, computer games, TV, and electronic conveniences have made it possible to avoid physical activity in our daily lives (see Figure 1.3)—they let us push grocery carts to gather food, ride cars for transportation, and push buttons to meet many other needs.

Our physical activity must keep in step with these changes. Most people today are not getting adequate exercise in their daily work and routines to combat the health problems associated with a lack of activity. This lack of activity gradually leads to reduced energy and vigor and eventually to health problems and diseases. Research (Blair et al., 1989) in recent years has shown a relationship between a lack of fitness and adult health problems, including degenerative cardiovascular diseases. Evidence (Gilliam, MacConnie, Geenen, Pels, & Freedson, 1982) indicates that these problems are already present and developing in childhood because many children are not developing the habits and values of an active lifestyle.

Developing a Commitment to Fitness

The challenge for our society is how to help children develop a lifetime commitment to physical fitness and a healthy lifestyle. If children are to be naturally motivated to be physically active, then the key is to start activity programs early, to make sure the activities are interesting to children, and to choose activities children can be successful at. Some ways to do this include providing education (information and knowledge about fitness and health-related issues); teaching children motor skills that enable them to participate in games, sports, gymnastics, dance, and fitness activities (see Belka, 1994; Buschner, 1994; Purcell, 1994; Werner, 1994); and providing developmentally appropriate and successful learning experiences so children develop competence and confidence in their physical abilities.

Physical education in school can have an impact on these goals, but others who affect children's lives, such as the classroom teacher and family members, must help. Classroom teachers and parents are extremely important and powerful role models. Classroom teachers can use learning experiences and activity sessions to increase children's knowledge and appreciation of the importance of fitness. Family exercise and health habits can have a major impact on children and reinforce, or unfortunately wash out, the lessons learned in physical education classes. For example, parents reinforce lessons on exercising for heart health when they exercise. On the other hand, the impact of a lesson on the harmful effects of smoking is negated when children see their parents smoking at home. Therefore, parents should be involved in children's fitness—they should receive up-to-date fitness information and participate with their children in fitness activities.

Figure 1.3 Modern conveniences lead to reduced physical activity in our daily lives.

Present Status of Children's Fitness

"Are children fit?" is a frequently asked question and the answers vary, depending on the criteria for fitness. One way to answer the question is to say that children have not had much time to become unfit! Compared to the adult population, children score higher on maximum oxygen consumption tests and have far less risk of cardiovascular disease, low back pain, and other problems due to deficiencies in fitness (Simons-Morton et al., 1987). On the other hand, if fitness test data (Ross & Gilbert, 1985) are used as criteria, then the status of children's fitness is not very encouraging. Data from the National Children and Youth Fitness Study II (NCYFS) (Ross & Pate, 1987) provide evidence that 6- to 9-year-old children carry more body fat than their counterparts of 20 or more years ago. In the same study a survey of activity levels found that approximately half of American youth are not getting the minimum weekly requirement of vigorous physical activity needed to maintain an effectively functioning cardiorespiratory system. So the key problem seems to be not that children don't score high enough on fitness tests, but the lack of regular vigorous physical activity in a high percentage of children.

In making a case to adults for regular exercise, the greatest appeal is the potential for a healthy, longer life. Using a similar strategy for children—convincing them that they should exercise to reduce their risk of atherosclerosis—is not a very effective strategy. The results of inactivity are not immediate; as with smoking or failing to brush teeth the problems develop gradually over time. This makes it difficult for children to realize the importance of these habits.

Another problem with convincing children to exercise is that even if children were "whipped" into magnificent shape, they would still have health risks as adults if they did not continue to exercise. The health effects of early activity and participation in sports and fitness do not carry over into adulthood unless regular vigorous activity continues to be part of a person's life. The standard phrase "use it or lose it" is appropriate—habits are necessary to maintain the health benefits of regular exercise. Habits are developed as a result of learning to value something highly enough to incorporate it into one's life. Valuing starts with information and successful experiences, and gradually develops into a sense that the experiences are important for the individual. This is why it makes sense to provide children with positive and successful experiences and to emphasize the enjoyment and immediate importance of physical activity.

How Children Benefit From Fitness Education

Physical activity presents an effective means of promoting good health and enhancing the quality of life (Seefeldt, 1986). The health benefits of exercise have been thoroughly documented and you can see some of the most relevant outcomes in Table 1.1. Diseases and health problems stemming from a lack of activity have origins early in life, so that is when an active lifestyle should be established. Fitness begins at birth and can continue throughout a person's life. The experiences children have in school make a lasting impression on them, negative or positive. Therefore, it is essential to conduct school programs well.

Young children should participate in daily physical activity and start hearing the message that activity is necessary for good health early. The school years offer a vital opportunity to mold the attitudes of children so they do not become inactive adults. Children need information about fitness, they need to start developing an understanding of fitness, and they need appropriate and successful fitness experiences. In short, they can develop positive attitudes and start to *value* fitness. Not all children have opportunities to participate in sports, dance, gymnastics, and recreational programs sponsored by the community. For these reasons physical education is one of the basic school subjects. It has an important role in providing all students opportunities to participate in and learn about regular physical activity. The National Association for Sport and Physical Education (NASPE) outlines the positive outcomes of quality physical education that help a child become "physically educated" (see Figure 1.4). These outcomes echo the benefits of regular vigorous activity and highlight the goals of skill development, activity enjoyment, and development of personal fitness programs.

The debate over national health insurance and the alarm over rising health costs demonstrates the need for preventive medicine. A physically fit lifestyle is an excellent example of preventive medicine. The alternative to a fit lifestyle is to increase the risk of heart disease, back pain, diabetes, osteoporosis, and obesity and to miss the positive physiological and psychological benefits of vigorous exercise. We have the opportunity to educate our youth about exercise and health habits that can improve

Counteracts major risk factors of heart disease (high blood pressure, obesity, and sedentary lifestyles)

Improves muscular strength, flexibility, and endurance

Improves self-confidence, self-esteem, and self-control

Helps regulate weight control, tones bodies, and improves body composition

Helps children establish and strive for achievable, personal goals

Helps students make appropriate decisions about their behavior and fitness

Helps students to follow rules and established procedures

Develops movement skills

Increases bone density

Helps release tension and anxiety

Strengthens peer relationships

Reduces risk of depression

Promotes a positive, lifelong attitude toward physical activity

Figure 1.4 Benefits of vigorous physical activity through quality physical education. *Note.* From *Fit to Achieve Through Quality, Daily Physical Education* by the National Association for Sport and Physical Education, 1987, Reston, VA: NASPE. Copyright 1987 by NASPE. Reprinted by permission of NASPE.

fitness and lower the risks of illness and disease. Because the benefits of regular and continuous activity extend beyond childhood, teaching fitness is an investment in the future well-being of both our children and society.

Goals and Approach to Teaching Fitness

The goals of teaching fitness to children are to help them acquire the skills, knowledge, and attitudes that lead to a lifetime of physical activity. Learning should occur in all three domains of human development—psychomotor, cognitive, and affective. Figure 1.5 lists some sample psychomotor, cognitive, and affective benchmarks related to physical fitness in a quality physical education program according to the NASPE Outcomes Committee (Franck et al., 1991). This book will describe learning experiences to help students achieve these benchmarks, which in turn help students become "physically educated."

Teaching fitness should be viewed as a long-term process of educating students about physical fitness and the importance of regular activity. The process starts out with achieving lower order objectives and gradually involves more complex, higher order objectives to guide students toward valuing fitness and becoming self-directed. Corbin (1987) refers to this process as the "stairway to lifetime fitness" (see Figure 1.6). Corbin points out, however, that just because children achieve a desirable level of fitness does not mean that they will maintain fitness for

a lifetime. Stimulating children to be active and achieve good levels of fitness in class is actually a lower order objective. Achieving higher order objectives such as planning and conducting their own personal fitness program is necessary before children can *value* physical fitness and make it an essential part of their lives. Simply pushing kids into shape so they score well on fitness tests may not result in developing positive feelings about exercise. To develop both the lower and higher order objectives that lead to participation in and valuing of an active lifestyle, the learning experiences in physical education should reflect the educational outcomes outlined by NASPE.

If training children to achieve high physical fitness scores was the primary objective of physical education programs, most teachers would not be able to meet the challenge because time for physical education is limited (Simons-Morton, O'Hara, Simons-Morton, & Parcel, 1987). Many programs only offer 30-minute physical education classes taught by a qualified specialist once or twice a week. With limited time and numerous objectives, the goal of "getting kids fit" during physical education class time is not realistic. Even if physical education is offered daily, the regimented fitness approach is not going to help children gain a cognitive understanding of fitness, will take time away from other important skill-related objectives, and will turn off many children from physical activity.

Performance on physical fitness tests is *not* the primary goal of teaching fitness in schools.

As a result of participating in a quality physical education program, it is reasonable to expect that the student will be able to do the following:

Psychomotor Domain (Has, Is, Does)

Sustain moderate physical activity (K, #16)

Participate daily in vigorous physical activity (K, #17)

Regularly participate in physical activity for the purpose of improving skillful performance and physical fitness (3-4, #17)

Move each joint through a full range of motion (1-2, #19)

Maintain continuous aerobic activity for a specific time (3-4, #14)

Participate in vigorous activity for a sustained period of time while maintaining a target heart rate (5-6, #12)

Recover from vigorous physical activity in an appropriate length of time (5-6, #13)

Monitor heart rate before, during, and after activity (5-6, #14)

Correctly demonstrate activities designed to improve and maintain muscular strength and endurance, flexibility, and cardiorespiratory functioning (5-6, #15)

Cognitive Domain (Knows)

Recognize that physical activity is good for personal well-being (K, #20)

Identify changes in the body during physical activity (e.g., function of the heart, circulatory and respiratory systems) (1-2, #25)

Describe healthful benefits that result from regular and appropriate participation in physical activity (3-4, #24)

Analyze potential risks associated with physical activities (3-4, #25)

Recognize that idealized images of the human body and performance as presented by the media may not be appropriate to imitate (5-6, #17)

Recognize that time and effort are prerequisites for skill improvement and fitness benefits (5-6, #18)

Identify opportunities in the school and community for regular participation in physical activity (5-6, #20)

Identify principles of training and conditioning for physical activity (e.g., overload and specificity principle; intensity, duration, and frequency) (5-6, #21)

Identify proper warm-up, conditioning, and cool-down techniques and the reason for using them (5-6, #22)

Identify benefits resulting from participation in different forms of physical activities (e.g., skill-related and health-related fitness components) (5-6, #23)

Affective Domain (Values)

Identify feelings that result from participation in physical activities (K, #22)

Accept the feelings resulting from challenges, successes, and failures in physical activity (1-2, #28)

Appreciate differences and similarities in others' physical activity (3-4, #27)

Enjoy the feeling resulting from involvement in physical activity (3-4, #29)

Celebrate personal successes and achievements and those of others (3-4, #30)

Choose to exercise at home for personal enjoyment and benefit (5-6, #28)

Figure 1.5 Sample benchmarks relevant for fitness. The first number in parentheses following each benchmark relates to the grade level that benchmark can be found under in the NASPE document; the second number gives the specific benchmark for that grade level. These will be referenced to objectives for learning experiences in Part II of this text, when appropriate. See page 49 for further information.

From *Physical Education Outcomes: A Project of the National Association for Sport and Physical Education* by M. Franck, G. Graham, H. Lawson, T. Loughrey, R. Ritson, M. Sanborn, and V. Seefeldt (The Outcomes Committee of NASPE), 1991. Adapted by permission of the National Association for Sport and Physical Education, Reston, VA.

Performance on fitness tests is the result of many factors that are out of control of teachers. Heredity, home habits including activity patterns and TV watching, parental exercise habits, parental exercise with children, and community opportunities all affect children's activity levels and fitness performances. A more realistic goal for physical education classes is to provide successful physical activities for children to help them develop skills and understand and value regular participation in physical activity so much that they can't do without it—they've got to have it!

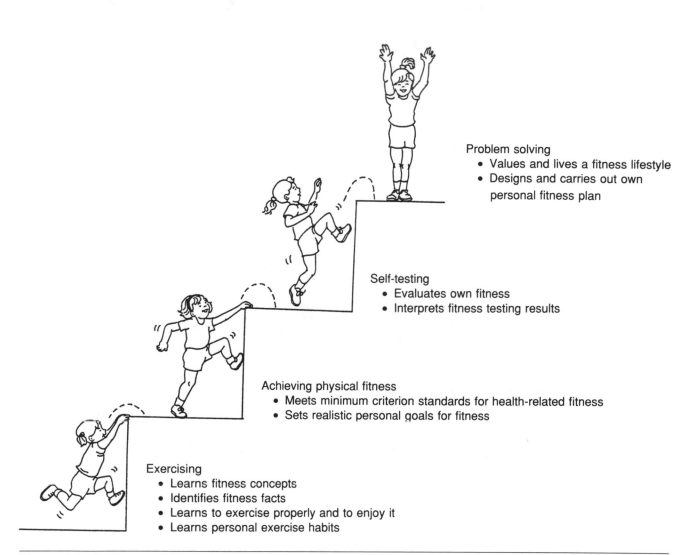

Problem solving
• Values and lives a fitness lifestyle
• Designs and carries out own
  personal fitness plan

Self-testing
• Evaluates own fitness
• Interprets fitness testing results

Achieving physical fitness
• Meets minimum criterion standards for health-related fitness
• Sets realistic personal goals for fitness

Exercising
• Learns fitness concepts
• Identifies fitness facts
• Learns to exercise properly and to enjoy it
• Learns personal exercise habits

Figure 1.6 Stairway to lifetime fitness. *Note.* From *Teaching Strategies for Improving Youth Fitness* (p. 47) by C.B. Corbin and R.P. Pangrazi, 1989, Dallas: Cooper Institute for Aerobics Research. Copyright 1989 by the Cooper Institute for Aerobics Research. Reprinted with permission of the Cooper Institute for Aerobics Research, Dallas, Texas.

Summary

This chapter has addressed why children need fitness education. Teaching fitness has evolved from simply doing activities with the assumption that children understand and are learning fitness concepts to planning specific learning experiences that focus on fitness information.

A quality physical education program should help children develop competence in the fundamental motor skills and concepts associated with games, gymnastics, and dance so they can participate successfully. The curriculum should also help children understand and value concepts of physical fitness and the contribution they make to a healthy lifestyle. Teaching children to be skillful movers and to be physically fit are complementary goals. Children should leave elementary school with knowledge, skills, and an intrinsic interest in maintaining a healthy lifestyle. The following chapters will provide strategies and learning experiences to accomplish these goals.

Chapter 2

Tailoring Fitness to Fit Your Teaching Situation

Teaching would be much easier if all schools and all grade levels were identical. Then a standardized curriculum with detailed lesson plans would work everywhere. The fact is, however, that our teaching situations have some similarities—and some definite differences! The differences include class size, facilities, class frequency, equipment, length of the class period, and a broad range of ages, abilities, and special needs within the same class of children. Figure 2.1 shows many of the factors that vary from one teaching environment to the next. This chapter briefly describes some ways the content in this book can be adapted to various teaching situations to best meet the needs of the children and also to heighten their enjoyment and learning.

Class Size

Although it is recommended that "physical education classes contain the same number of children as the classrooms (e.g., 25 children per class)" (Council on Physical Education for Children, 1992), some schools and districts schedule two or more classes at the same time, which means the PE teacher must teach 60 or more children simultaneously. Although this makes the teacher's job difficult, there are ways that teachers can develop the content to provide children with positive (albeit far from ideal) learning experiences. For example, the use of stations, or learning centers, is probably one of the more efficient ways to organize large groups of children (Graham, 1992). And using written directions can minimize the time spent talking to the children, who often seem less inclined to listen when they are in large groups. Also, the teacher must devote substantial time to teaching management routines (Siedentop, 1991) or protocols (Graham, 1992) so that classes are run efficiently with minimal interruptions. Establishing a routine for immediate activity (jumping rope, climbing on playground equipment, practicing individual stretching exercises) is recommended (Graham, 1992). Signalling devices from whistles to battery operated megaphones are helpful at various times to communicate directions. Another idea is to use videotape instruction (see Figure 2.2) so you can circulate throughout the class.

Equipment

One reason why large class sizes are *not* recommended is that most physical education programs do not have sufficient equipment—even for 25 or 30 children. Consequently, if teachers are not careful, the children spend considerable time waiting for turns rather than actually moving. But innovative teachers have discovered ways to maximize

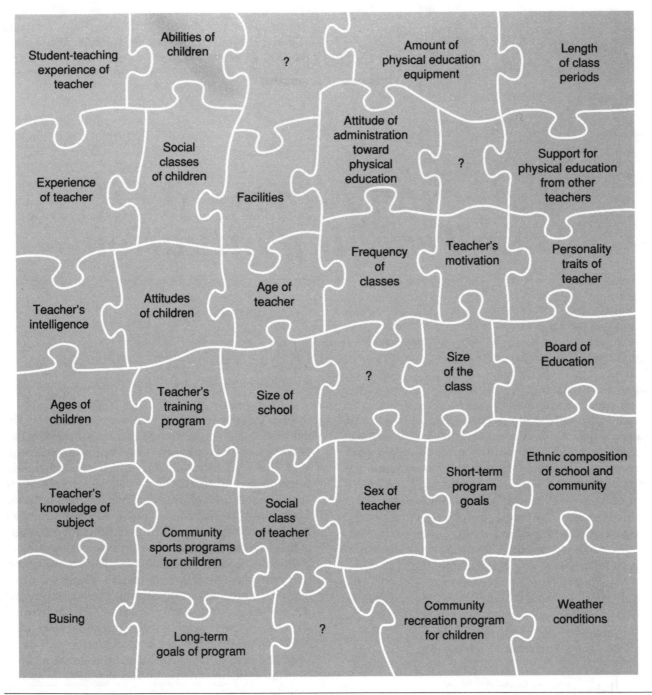

Figure 2.1 Interacting factors that contribute to the unique ecology of each school. *Note.* From *Children Moving* (p. 8) by G. Graham, S. Holt/Hale, and M. Parker, 1987, Mountain View, CA: Mayfield Publishing. Copyright 1987 by Mayfield Publishing. Reprinted by permission.

practice opportunities for children, even with limited equipment. Plastic milk bottles or bleach bottles filled with sand and bicycle inner tube material can be used as light resistance for muscular strength and endurance activities. Carpet squares can sometimes substitute for expensive mats. Equipment that is used only occasionally, such as stethoscopes, can be borrowed.

Facilities

Although some teachers have adequate indoor and outdoor space, others are less fortunate. In fact, some teachers have no indoor space whatsoever. Others have no grassy areas. Following are some ideas and suggestions for how the content in this book can be adapted for limited indoor or outdoor

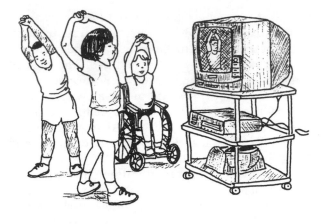

Figure 2.2   Using videotape instruction.

space. Fitness content can be taught in almost any situation with some adaptations. Because visual presentations (see Figure 2.3) are so helpful yet most teachers do not have a permanent space to set up materials and teaching aids, you may have to make such adjustments as carrying a poster board or easel to class, making laminated posters, or using a small chalkboard or erasable board (available from school supply or department stores). You can write signs on paper with felt markers and tape them on cones with masking tape or make fold-out signs by hinging two pieces of wood together and stapling the signs on the wood. Convenient weighted sign materials are also available from equipment manufacturers. You can put up bulletin boards and chalkboards in any available space, even in places such as the cafeteria or in hallways.

Inclement weather means teaching in class-rooms, cafeterias, and hallways (see Figure 2.4). Many teachers take advantage of the cafeteria space by getting the school to purchase portable

tables that can be moved quickly. Many learning experiences require paper and pencil. We recommend that you use clipboards and heavy 4 × 6 or 5 × 8 file cards, and stay out of the wind or don't use paper and pencil on windy days!

A lesson such as the Heart Pump Circuit (see chapter 7) will not be possible unless you can set up the environment prior to the class. A stage, all-purpose room, or unused classroom or trailer are possible sites. Other lessons such as the Health-Related Circuit (see chapter 6) will have to be modified to suit limited spaces. You might have all the children do the same activity in the classroom instead of using stations that take up more space. You will have to use activities that can be performed in personal space near desks or in small areas (see Figure 2.4). Instead of using jumping rope for an aerobic activity, you could substitute chair stepping for the classroom setting.

Class Frequency and Length

Schools and classes differ in the number of days per week that the children attend physical education classes and the length of the classes. Children who have physical education every day for 30 minutes can be expected to learn more than children who only have 60 minutes of physical education each week. This is one reason it is virtually impossible to suggest a standardized physical education curriculum. As suggested in the section later in this chapter on planning, you will need to consider these factors as you plan. Aim to organize and teach your classes so that if students have physical education twice a week for 30 minutes, they receive more than 16 hours of actual learning time each year (Kelly, 1989).

Figure 2.3   Using visual aids.

Figure 2.4   Teaching in the classroom.

The amount of time you have children in class is a major determining factor for the content area of fitness—the number of class meetings will influence decisions about what and how to teach. Meeting every day will give students regular opportunities to participate in fitness activities and to learn fitness concepts. Meeting only once a week, however, will mean choosing a limited number of fitness concepts to cover during the year.

Limited class time with children will also mean that other ways to motivate learning of fitness concepts and participation in fitness activities will have to come outside of scheduled physical education time. The Fitness Club (see chapter 7) and Home Exercise Program (see chapter 5, page 43) are good ways to encourage children to participate in out-of-class activities. Although out-of-class activities are very important for all teaching situations, it is essential for programs that have minimal contact time with students.

Accommodating Individual Differences

Remember that the American Master Teacher Program series takes a child-centered approach (Graham, 1992). Learning experiences are not rigid or cast in stone. They are dynamic and can be changed and modified based on teacher observations of individual children's needs. This is in contrast to a subject-centered approach that treats all children as if they have the same abilities and learn at the same rates.

Many classes today have children with special needs who are mainstreamed (i.e., their physical education class is scheduled with another class). In some instances you can accommodate children with special needs (not only those who are mainstreamed), by techniques such as *teaching by invitation* or *intratask variation* (Graham, 1992). In other instances it may be necessary to make different adaptations to meet the needs of these students. Some accommodations that teachers can make for children when teaching physical fitness are discussed in this section.

A peer-tutor or buddy system can be an effective strategy for students with disabilities. For example, partially sighted or blind students can be helped by a sighted partner during fitness testing and fitness learning experiences. During walking and running activities, the visually-impaired student can use a position on the side and hold the arm of the sighted partner.

Students in wheelchairs will function best on smooth surfaces. Students with mental retardation should be given structured activities, and cognitive information will have to be modified. The Special Olympics Program can be used to encourage regular participation in fitness and motor activities. Some physical fitness batteries are adapted for students with special needs. Contact the American Alliance for Health, Physical Education, Recreation and Dance for information.

Invariably there are obese children in our classes. Forcing them to straggle in last with everyone else watching them complete the mile fitness test is cruel and humiliating. You can have them perform the test privately at another time or run only half a mile to prevent the unnecessary humiliation. Any distance running will mean that some students will finish last, however. One solution is to measure running events by time—everyone performs their best effort for a specified period of time and all finish at the same time. A good example of this is to have students run as far as they can for 9 minutes rather than running a mile for time.

Students' Level of Experience

The amount of students' previous instruction on fitness topics will determine the type of learning experiences you plan and implement. Occasionally you may have a group of kindergarten children who progress through the primary learning experiences and by second grade are ready for more advanced lessons. You could modify the primary lessons and try some intermediate lessons, but recognize that 7- and 8-year-old children may not be cognitively ready for the higher order thinking that is required in some lessons. More frequently you will probably encounter intermediate classes that lack experience in fitness concepts. These classes should start with the primary learning experiences. For example, if fourth-grade students have not had instruction about the heart, then they would benefit from primary learning experiences before going on to more advanced lessons.

Children's Maturity Level

The maturity and learning readiness skills of a class will determine what fitness learning experiences you teach and how you teach them. Some children and classes are more ready to take responsibility for learning—some have good work skills and some don't. In several of the learning experiences, the use of task cards and learning centers requires that students are willing and able to follow procedures and stay on-task without direct teacher supervision. When trying these new teaching strategies and others such as partner self-testing and guided discovery, expect to teach the procedures and to have a period of adjustment. We recommend that you try a new lesson idea with one of your most cooperative and mature classes first before using it with other classes.

Planning

Chapter 3 contains an overview of the content that can be developed through the learning experiences in chapters 6 to 10. An important decision you must make as a teacher is how much of the content described in this book to use in your program. Remember, this is only one of the five books (Belka, 1994; Buschner, 1994; Purcell, 1994; Werner, 1994) that describe the content of physical education for children. Ideally, your program will include content from each of the areas, so you have some difficult decisions to make. A complete outline for planning is provided in *Teaching Children Physical Education* (Graham, 1992), but only you can develop the plans that will work best at your school. Also included in this book are benchmarks (Franck et al., 1991) that relate specifically to this content area. Use these benchmarks to help decide which aspects of the content are most important for your children to learn (see Figure 1.5).

Another important planning factor is the length of time you have taught the children. Your plans will (and should) be different for the first year of a program than for the tenth year. When you have worked with fifth or sixth graders from the time they started school, they will be able to do, and will know, different things than the fifth and sixth graders did your first year at that school. If you are new to a school or have not taught fitness concepts, then you should start by teaching the basic fitness information described in chapter 3. On the other hand, if you have taught fitness concepts to your students for several years then you can go beyond basic factual information and get involved in more complex learning experiences. Because fitness relates to all the other aspects of the curriculum you should integrate it into lessons throughout the year, emphasizing the benefits of dance, gymnastics, and game activities for improving fitness and health.

Teacher's Knowledge of Exercise Physiology

The emphasis and quality of fitness instruction also depend on knowledge of exercise physiology. Teachers with a strong background in this field can use their knowledge to break complex information into smaller parts and design learning experiences that match students' readiness and cognitive development. This book provides practical, simplified information about physical fitness that is developmentally appropriate for children. It does not, however, present the in-depth knowledge behind these concepts. We highly recommend attending inservice workshops and reading the selections in the "Suggested Readings" that provide up-to-date exercise physiology and fitness information.

Summary

One of the most valid criticisms of physical education programs has been that they were designed only for athletes—and were a painful experience for those who were poorly skilled. Contemporary physical educators are moving away from this one-model-fits-all pattern of restrictive physical education toward programs that are adjusted, adapted, and designed specifically to match the abilities, interests, and needs of individual children. This chapter describes some considerations that contemporary teachers take into account when designing programs specifically for the children at their schools.

Chapter 3

Incorporating Fitness Into Your Program

Most physical education programs include some fitness exercises such as sit-ups, push-ups, stretching exercises, jumping jacks, and running laps. Children may participate in these activities throughout the year or as part of a regular warm-up routine. Regular participation in fitness activities in class is important, but teaching fitness should not stop there. Children also need information about why they are doing the activities. Integrating knowledge and fitness activities will help children begin to value physical fitness and make physical activity a regular part of their lives.

A balanced physical fitness curriculum includes content relevant to the psychomotor, cognitive, and affective domains. The fitness curriculum should include skills (what children will demonstrate), knowledge (what children will know), and attitudes (what children will value) associated with a physically fit lifestyle. Because time for physical education is limited in most schools and the potential curriculum content is extensive, careful planning is necessary to cover the most important objectives.

To help you plan a comprehensive and developmentally appropriate curriculum, the fitness learning experiences that children should have in physical education classes are organized into the following five categories and presented in five chapters in Part II (see Figure 3.1):

1. Introducing fitness concepts
2. Cardiorespiratory endurance
3. Muscular strength and endurance
4. Flexibility
5. Healthy habits and wellness

Each of the five chapters includes important information that should be taught from pre-kindergarten through sixth grade. Some of the content is most appropriate to introduce at the primary level, pre-kindergarten through second grade.

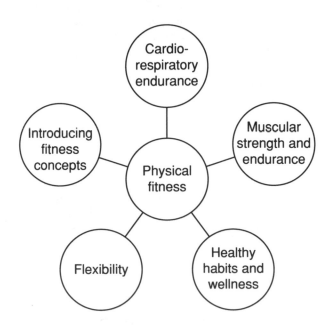

Figure 3.1   Fitness curriculum categories.

Other content is best suited for the intermediate level, third through sixth grades. Learning experiences in the intermediate grades should build on information presented in the primary lessons. At the intermediate level, children should bring more experience and cognitive ability to interpret and apply the information. Therefore, the fitness concepts in this chapter are each divided into two sections: primary (pre-K–2), and intermediate (3–6).

This chapter provides basic physical fitness information and an outline of the important topics that should be presented in the pre-K through sixth-grade physical education curriculum. Keep in mind that the choice of learning experiences for your particular class will depend on a number of factors mentioned in chapter 2. Also consider that the total physical fitness curriculum includes the fitness content and activities that are taught in regular classroom settings and out of school as well as in physical education classes. This chapter describes the background information that children should receive from all these sources and provides a list of the important fitness concepts for each of the five fitness curriculum categories.

Introducing Fitness Concepts

Your introduction to fitness concepts should explain the meaning of physical fitness, indicate activities that promote good fitness and those that don't (and explain why), and provide guidelines to maintain and improve fitness.

Physical fitness describes the capacity of the body to function efficiently and effectively during work, play, and in emergencies. Optimal physical fitness is necessary to work effectively, to enjoy leisure time, to be healthy, to resist hypokinetic diseases (high blood pressure, obesity, heart disease), and to meet emergencies. There are two types of physical fitness, health-related and skill-related. Health-related fitness includes cardiorespiratory fitness, flexibility, muscular endurance and strength, and body composition. Skill-related fitness includes agility, balance, coordination, power, reaction time, and speed. Physical fitness, then, is not a single characteristic; it combines many characteristics. To help children develop an active, physically fit lifestyle, you should provide opportunities to develop adequate levels of each of the health-related and skill-related components.

Health-Related Fitness Components

Cardiorespiratory fitness refers to the ability of the heart, blood vessels, blood, and respiratory system to supply fuel, especially oxygen, to the muscles and to the ability of large muscle groups to utilize fuel to perform exercise continuously for an extended period of time. Flexibility is defined as the range of motion in the muscles, tendons, and ligaments surrounding a joint. Muscular endurance refers to the ability of the muscles to repeatedly contract and work over a period of time, whereas muscular strength is the ability to exert a maximum external force or to lift a heavy weight. Body composition is the relative amount of fat and lean body weight (muscle, bone, and other fat-free tissue) that makes up the body.

Skill-Related Fitness Components

Skill-related fitness refers to physical components necessary for the successful execution of various sports skills. Agility is the ability to rapidly and accurately change the direction of the entire body in space. Dodging a tagger requires good agility. Balance is the maintenance of equilibrium while stationary or while moving. Performing movements on a balance beam requires good balance. Coordination refers to the ability to use sensory information to perform motor tasks smoothly and accurately. Juggling, hitting a baseball, catching a ball, and kicking a ball are examples of activities requiring good coordination. Another skill-related fitness component is power—the ability to transfer energy into force at a fast rate. A vertical jump requires considerable power. Reaction time is the amount of time it takes to react to a stimulus. Starting a sprint race requires good reaction time. Speed is the ability to perform a movement in a short period of time. Playing a game of tag successfully or outrunning a player in soccer requires speed.

Benefits of Fitness

This book focuses on the health-related components of fitness, those components that are necessary to promote good health and optimal physical development and that are positively influenced by regular physical activity. The other American Master Teacher content books (Belka, 1994; Buschner, 1994; Purcell, 1994; and Werner, 1994) provide learning experiences that emphasize the skill-related fitness components. Health-related and skill-related fitness components are equally important for children.

Present the benefits of participation in regular exercise to children using vocabulary appropriate to their cognitive level and experience. Some of the important benefits are that exercise

- makes the heart a stronger pump;
- helps lower blood pressure and resting and working heart rates;
- reduces the risks of heart disease;
- strengthens muscles and bones;
- gives more energy for daily activities;
- helps maintain a normal body weight;
- provides greater efficiency for work and play; and
- reduces stress and tension.

Principles for Maintaining and Improving Physical Fitness

It is important to follow several principles to safely participate in exercise and obtain the benefits of physical activity. The principles of overload, frequency, intensity, time, specificity, and progression are introduced in this section and are referred to later when discussing safe and beneficial exercise procedures for each of the components of health-related fitness.

- *Overload*—This term refers to the principle of doing more exercise than usual in order to stimulate higher levels of fitness. To improve any of the physical fitness components you can apply the principle of overload by increasing the frequency, intensity, or time of the exercise. These three factors are referred to by the acronym FIT. *F* stands for *frequency*—how often to exercise. Research indicates that daily physical activity is desirable, and specific exercises in the various health-related components should be performed at least 3 days per week. *I* stands for *intensity*—how hard to exercise. Children will benefit from exercise that is hard enough to require exertion. Elevating heart rate, stretching a joint through the full range of motion, and taking full weight on the hands are examples of intensity of exercise. *T* stands for *time*—how long should be spent doing an activity or exercise. For example, 20 to 60 minutes of continuous aerobic activity is necessary for improving cardiorespiratory endurance.

The specific FIT requirements vary for each fitness component. For example, daily frequent, mild, whole-body activity is necessary for the component of body composition, whereas shorter bouts of periodic exercises improve muscular strength and endurance. Many health benefits of exercise occur at levels less than those needed for athletic performance. Intense training routines are not required to achieve healthy levels in the fitness components, but regular physical activity that meets the FIT criteria is necessary.

- *Specificity*—To develop a particular aspect of fitness, you must do activities that are specific to that fitness component. For example, strength-building exercises such as push-ups will increase arm and shoulder muscular strength and endurance, but will do little to improve cardiorespiratory fitness. The principle of specificity also refers to the development of specific body parts. Push-ups will develop arm and shoulder muscles, but not the leg muscles.

- *Progression*—The frequency, intensity, and time of exercise should be increased gradually to match an individual's present state of fitness. Slow progression will help prevent the soreness, injury, and frustration that may occur with trying to do too much all at once. Present fitness level, genetic background, body structure, health habits, and even motivation will vary between individuals, so all of these differences must be considered when applying the FIT principle.

Fitness Tests

Fitness tests give us a measurement of how physically fit or "in shape" the body is. Different fitness tests are used to help us evaluate the physical condition of different components of fitness. The 1-mile run for time or 9-minute run for distance is used to measure cardiorespiratory fitness. Abdominal muscular strength and endurance is measured by the 60-second modified sit-up test. Upper body strength and endurance is measured by the modified pull-up, pull-up, or flexed-arm hang. Flexibility of the lower back and hamstring muscles is measured by the sit-and-reach test. Body composition is evaluated by using the triceps and calf skinfold measurements. Although these tests are widely used, there are questions about how well they measure certain fitness components. Revisions have been made and will continue to be made as more accurate information is discovered.

Primary Level Fitness Concepts

After you have introduced fitness concepts at the primary level (grades pre-K–2), children should be able to

- explain the meaning of being "fit" or "in shape";
- identify the importance of being active;
- identify and perform activities that are fun and promote body fitness;

- identify parts of the body that keep us fit (heart, lungs, blood vessels, muscles, kidneys, bones);
- demonstrate correct walking and running form;
- explain and demonstrate the meaning of pacing; and
- perform procedures for warming up and cooling down.

Intermediate Level Fitness Concepts

After you have introduced fitness concepts, students at the intermediate level (grades 3–6) should be able to

- review concepts introduced at the primary level;
- define physical fitness;
- identify components of health-related and skill-related fitness and perform activities associated with each component;
- perform skill-related (stand long jump, agility run, 50-yard dash, and balance beam) and health-related (1-mile run, 9-minute run, push-ups, sit-ups, modified pull-ups, and sit-and-reach) self-testing activities;
- identify the purpose of physical fitness tests, participate in fitness testing, set personal goals for fitness maintenance or improvement, and assess progress; and
- identify the principles of training and conditioning to maintain and improve physical fitness, which are

  frequency,
  intensity,
  time,
  overload,
  specificity, and
  progression.

Cardiorespiratory Endurance

This category includes information about the heart and circulatory system, the lungs and respiratory system, and the relationship of exercise to a healthy cardiorespiratory system. Cardiorespiratory endurance is considered the most important component of health-related physical fitness because it contributes so closely to positive health benefits. Regular cardiorespiratory exercise helps reduce many of the risk factors associated with sedentary living.

Aerobic Activity

Aerobic (meaning with oxygen) endurance is another term used to describe cardiorespiratory endurance. Aerobic exercises are whole-body activities involving large-muscle groups that are continuous and last for an extended period of time. Examples are brisk walking, running, bicycling, swimming, cross-country skiing, and dance. Other activities such as games and gymnastics can be aerobic if participation is vigorous, continuous, and produces a heart rate within the target range. Good aerobic or cardiorespiratory fitness means that the heart, lungs, and blood vessels are able to function efficiently to deliver nutrients and oxygen to the tissues and remove waste products.

Cardiorespiratory endurance requires the fitness of the heart, circulatory system, and lungs. The heart—a pear-shaped muscle approximately the size of a fist located just left of the middle chest—must get regular, progressive exercise like any other muscle to maintain or increase strength. The heart never rests and beats an average of 120,000 times each day, pumping 5,000 to 6,000 quarts of blood every 12 hours. A larger and more powerful heart will be able to pump more blood with each stroke (or increase its stroke volume), thus becoming more efficient.

Vascular System

The vascular system includes the arteries, veins, and capillaries (see Figure 3.2). Healthy arteries are elastic tubes that expand to permit the free flow of blood. Arteries may be damaged due to atherosclerosis, which reduces their internal diameter because of deposits of fatty substances on their interior walls, or they may have hardened, nonelastic walls (see Figure 3.3). The coronary arteries are very important to good heart function because they provide the blood to the heart.

Veins are tubes that carry the oxygen-depleted blood filled with waste products back to the heart. Veins have thinner, less elastic walls than arteries and contain small valves to prevent the backward flow of blood. Because veins are intertwined in the muscle tissue, movement of the skeletal muscles assists the return of the blood to the heart. Capillaries are very thin and nearly invisible vessels. They serve as transfer stations where oxygen and nutrients are released and waste products are removed from the tissues. Veins receive blood from the capillaries for the return trip to the heart.

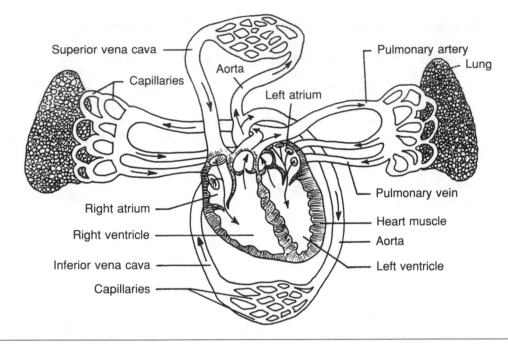

Figure 3.2 Heart and circulatory system.

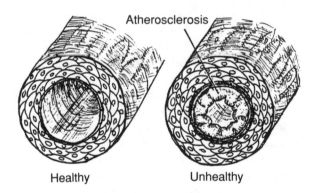

Figure 3.3 Healthy and unhealthy arteries.

Respiratory System

Respiration describes the process of taking in oxygen through the nose or mouth and delivering it to the lungs, where it is picked up by the blood. Delivering oxygen from the blood to the tissues takes place through capillaries and is called internal respiration. Breathing increases during exercise to provide more oxygen to the blood and working muscles. An efficient, healthy aerobic system requires fitness of both the external and internal respiratory systems.

The lungs are two pinkish air sacs located inside the chest. They are like balloons, filling up and losing air when a person breathes in and out. Air contains oxygen, the energy or fuel for the muscles. Just as a car needs gas, the muscles need oxygen.

The blood picks up oxygen in the lungs and carries it to the heart. Oxygen-rich blood is bright red in color. The heart pumps the oxygen-rich blood to the muscles of the body to make energy. After the blood gives up the oxygen and picks up waste products including carbon dioxide, it returns to the heart. The heart then pumps the blood to the lungs to get rid of the carbon dioxide and pick up fresh oxygen. This cycle continuously repeats itself.

Target Heart Rate

The pulse is caused by a rush of blood through the arteries after each heartbeat. The pulse can be felt on the radial artery in the wrist or on the carotid artery of the neck. Use the index finger, middle finger, or both to take the pulse—do not use the thumb because it has a pulse of its own. Heart rate (HR) is the number of times the heart beats in 1 minute. Resting heart rate (RHR) is the number of times the heart beats in 1 minute when the body is completely relaxed. The maximum heart rate (MHR) is the maximum number of times the heart can beat in 1 minute. The MHR is estimated to be 220 minus a person's age in years. For example, a 10-year-old's MHR is approximately 210 beats per minute. A person cannot exercise for very long at MHR, so it is beneficial to exercise in the target heart rate range (THR)—60% to 80% of the MHR. For example, a 10-year-old's THR is calculated as:

$$60\% \text{ of MHR} = .60 \times 210 = 126$$
$$80\% \text{ of MHR} = .80 \times 210 = 168$$

Therefore, the THR for a 10-year-old would be between 126 and 168 beats per minute. Exercise within the target heart rate range is necessary to improve cardiorespiratory fitness. This is the intensity (I) component of the FIT principle to maintain and improve cardiorespiratory fitness. Frequency (F) refers to how often exercise at the target rate should be conducted, and time (T) refers to the duration of exercise at the target heart rate. Daily activity at target heart rate for 15 minutes or more is recommended for children to meet the FIT prescription for cardiorespiratory endurance.

Measuring Cardiorespiratory Endurance

Distance runs, the 1-mile run/walk test, and the 9-minute run/walk test measure cardiorespiratory maximal functional capacity and endurance. For the 1-mile run/walk students are instructed to run and walk at the fastest pace they can sustain for the entire distance and a time is recorded for the score. For the 9-minute run/walk students go at their fastest pace for the entire time period and the total distance they covered is recorded as the score. The half-mile and 6-minute run can be substitutes for young children. The advantage of the timed distance runs versus the set distance runs is that all children finish at the same time, whereas a disadvantage is that recording the distance each student covers requires more organization.

Criterion scores and percentile norms are available for comparing your students' scores with national standards. Criterion-referenced standards provide scores that indicate the minimum levels established for good health. Percentile norms are used to compare students with other children of the same age and gender. The use of these procedures varies depending on which fitness testing program is used. See chapter 5 for a list of the most popular fitness testing programs. We recommend using criterion-referenced standards to encourage children to meet healthy standards and improve their personal goals.

Primary Level Fitness Concepts

In regard to cardiorespiratory fitness, primary students (grades pre-K–2) should be able to

- identify location, size, and function of the heart;
- identify parts and function of the circulatory and respiratory systems;
- identify where to find their heartbeat;
- identify the effects of rest and exercise on the heart;
- identify activities and habits that don't help the heart;
- perform activities that do help the heart—healthy heart activities; and
- understand how to measure a strong heart (endurance challenges including the 1-mile run/walk or 9-minute run/walk).

Intermediate Level Fitness Concepts

In regard to cardiorespiratory fitness, intermediate students (grades 3–6) should be able to

- review primary concepts;
- identify the meaning of cardiorespiratory fitness and "aerobics";
- identify the definition of endurance;
- participate in regular aerobic endurance activities;
- identify the benefits of high levels of cardiorespiratory endurance;
- identify how the heart, lungs, vascular system, and respiratory system respond to exercise;
- identify the role of oxygen in producing energy;
- demonstrate the ability to count the pulse and calculate heart rate;
- evaluate the contribution of a variety of physical activities to cardiorespiratory fitness;
- identify the risk factors of heart disease and ways to modify the risk factors;
- identify how to measure cardiorespiratory fitness and the purpose of the endurance tests (1-mile and 9-minute run/walk); and
- perform safe procedures for warm-up before and cool-down after aerobic exercise.

Muscular Strength and Endurance

This category includes information about the muscles and how to improve muscular strength and endurance. Muscular strength and endurance are two separate, but interrelated, fitness components. Muscular strength is the largest amount of force one can produce with a single maximal effort, for example, lifting up a heavy mat. Muscular endurance is the capacity of a group of muscles to continue working for a long period of time. Good muscular endurance enables a person to hold a position or repeat a movement without getting tired, as you would when using your hands on the playground bars to suspend your body off the ground or when performing many sit-ups or modified push-ups.

Muscles are made up of millions of tiny fibers. The fibers in each muscle are grouped into motor units and each motor unit is connected by nerve pathways to the brain. The brain signals the muscles to indicate how many motor units are needed to perform various tasks. For example, more motor units are required to lift a mat than to lift a beanbag. The muscle fibers get larger when they are exercised regularly.

During childhood up to about age 12 and the onset of puberty, boys and girls have the potential to develop similar gains in strength and endurance. After puberty the hormone testosterone enables males to make greater increases in muscle size. However, both sexes can always benefit from equal opportunities to increase their muscular strength and endurance.

Principles for Developing Muscular Strength and Endurance

Children should participate in muscular strength and endurance activities on a regular basis by following the principles of overload, frequency, intensity, time, specificity, and progression. Overloading the muscles by moving a weight or the resistance of the body is needed to maintain and improve muscular strength and endurance. The FIT principle can be applied by exercising the major muscle groups of the body at least twice a week. To improve both muscular strength and endurance 8 to 12 repetitions of light weights or resistance that causes fatigue is recommended. Using heavy weights that require a maximum or nearly maximum effort to move them one time are not necessary and could cause injury. Activities that involve moving one's own body weight, such as doing cartwheels or climbing on playground bars, are also recommended to help children develop muscular strength and endurance.

Exercise designs should follow other principles, such as progression and specificity, to develop muscular strength and endurance. The time and intensity of the activities and exercises should increase gradually (progression), and exercises should be specific to a particular muscle group to increase the strength and endurance (specificity). For example, curl-ups will help develop the abdominal muscles, whereas push-ups are necessary for arm and shoulder development. Repetitions means the number of times an exercise is consecutively repeated. Exercises are often done in sets of a specific number of repetitions. For example, two sets of 10 repetitions indicates that students will perform the exercise

10 times, rest briefly, and perform the exercise 10 times again.

Activities That Improve Muscular Strength and Endurance

Isotonic exercises mean that the muscle changes length and the resistance moves—lifting jugs filled with sand is an example. Isometric exercises are muscle contractions in which the muscle remains the same length. For example, force is applied against an immovable object, as in forcefully pressing the hands together. In physical education classes activities such as taking the body weight on the hands (cartwheels, handstands), suspending the body and climbing on playground equipment, jumping and landing, push-ups, and sit-ups will help children develop their muscular strength and endurance (Figure 3.4).

Measuring Muscular Strength and Endurance

Several tests are used for measuring muscular strength and endurance for the upper body and abdominal muscle groups. Abdominal strength and endurance is evaluated by performing repeated sit-ups for 1 minute. Students lie on their backs with knees flexed and feet flat on the floor and held stable by a partner. They cross their arms on the chest with hands held on the opposite shoulders. The up position is complete when elbows touch the thighs and the down position is complete when the midback makes contact with the surface.

Pull-ups, modified pull-ups, and the flexed-arm hang are tests used to measure upper body muscular strength and endurance. Regular pull-ups are

Figure 3.4 Muscle strength and endurance activities.

used to evaluate arm and shoulder girdle strength and endurance. Students begin by using an overhand (palms outward) grip with legs and arms fully extended. From the hanging position the body must be raised with the arms until the chin is positioned over the bar. The total number of pull-ups completed without touching feet to the floor is used as the measurement. Because many elementary children do not have the arm strength to lift their entire body weight, we recommend using the modified pull-up for all children (Figure 3.5). The students lie directly underneath a low bar with arms completely extended so the upper back is several inches off the floor. They use their arms to pull the body up toward the bar so the chest touches the bar and repeat this motion as many times as possible to achieve a final score. Another test for the arm and shoulder muscles is the flexed-arm hang. A student holds a horizontal bar with the palms facing away, suspending the body with the chin positioned above the bar. The score is the number of seconds the position is held without resting the chin on the bar. National criterion scores and percentile norms for these tests vary slightly depending on the fitness testing program that is used. See chapter 5 for a list of the most popular programs.

Primary Level Fitness Concepts

In regard to muscular strength and endurance primary students (grades pre-K–2) should be able to

- identify that the body has many muscles,
- identify the purpose of muscles,
- identify correct procedures for lifting objects,
- perform activities and exercises to achieve strong muscles,

Figure 3.5   Modified pull-up.

- identify and practice appropriate exercises and activities for specific groups of muscles, and
- learn to correctly perform exercises using their own body weight as resistance.

Intermediate Level Fitness Concepts

In regard to muscular strength and endurance intermediate students (grades 3–6) should be able to

- review primary concepts,
- identify and locate major muscles,
- identify the meaning and importance of muscular strength and endurance,
- perform exercises and activities for specific muscle groups that improve muscular strength and endurance,
- describe how to apply the principle of overload by using repetitions and sets, and
- identify how to measure muscular strength and endurance (explaining the purpose of the sit-up, modified pull-up, flexed-arm hang, and regular pull-up tests).

Flexibility

In a good fitness program the teacher presents information to help students understand the meaning of flexibility, why it is important, and how to stretch safely. Flexibility is the range of motion in a joint and its surrounding muscles. The range of motion means that the muscles, tendons, and ligaments surrounding the joint can bend or flex. Good flexibility helps the body move freely and also helps prevent injury. Although there is no absolute standard for flexibility, failure to exercise the joints regularly through the full range of motion can lead to tightening and shortening the muscles, tendons, and ligaments.

Static stretching, as opposed to ballistic (bouncing) stretching, is recommended for safety reasons. To increase flexibility, the muscle must be stretched beyond its normal length, but *not* to the point of pain. Tell students to stretch until they feel a slight discomfort. Then hold the stretched position for 10 to 30 seconds. When a muscle is stretched too far, or too quickly as in bouncing, a nerve reflex, called the *stretch reflex*, responds by sending a signal to the muscles, telling them to contract. This helps prevent muscle injury. Proper stretching should be slow and gradual to the point of mild tension. Muscles should be warmed up with general, whole-body exercises before engaging in stretching.

Guidelines for Safe Stretching

Following the FIT principle is important to improve flexibility, just as it is for the other health-related fitness components. Encourage daily stretching activities to maintain and improve flexibility (frequency). Intensity (I) means stretching until mild tension is felt, and time (T) refers to holding the stretched position for 10 to 30 seconds. Other principles that apply to flexibility are overload (stretching to the point of mild discomfort) and progression (holding each stretch 5 to 10 seconds at first and working up to holding each stretch 20 or 30 seconds). The principle of specificity applies to flexibility as well as to muscular strength and endurance—to maintain or increase the flexibility of a particular muscle group or joint, the muscles in that specific part must be stretched regularly. For example, exercises aimed at increasing the flexibility of the leg muscles will have no effect upon the flexibility of the arms and shoulders.

Measuring Flexibility

Although measuring the degree of flexibility is specific to each joint in the body, the sit-and-reach test is commonly used to evaluate the flexibility of the lower back and hamstring muscles (Figure 3.6). Students remove their shoes and sit with their knees fully extended and their heels flat against the measuring device. They extend their arms forward with the hands on top of each other and lean forward, extending the fingertips and palms as far forward as possible. Four trials are taken and the most distant point reached on the fourth trial by both hands and held for 1 second is used as the score. The score is invalid and the test should be readministered if the student fails to keep the knees fully extended or if the hands reach unevenly. National standards used for comparison can be found in the fitness programs listed in chapter 5.

Figure 3.6   Sit-and-reach test.

Primary Level Fitness Concepts

For flexibility primary students (grades pre-K–2) should be able to

- identify the meaning of stretching and
- identify and perform the correct procedures for safe stretching.

Intermediate Level Fitness Concepts

For flexibility intermediate students (grades 3–6) should be able to

- review primary concepts,
- identify the meaning of flexibility,
- explain the relationship between stretching and the body's joints,
- identify the benefits and importance of stretching,
- perform exercises to improve flexibility using safe exercises and correct procedures, and
- identify how to measure flexibility (the purpose of the sit-and-reach test).

Healthy Habits and Wellness

This category includes information associated with body composition, caloric balance, nutrition, personal health habits, and behavior management strategies that can help children develop habits that contribute to health and well-being. Many concepts in this category should be addressed as part of the regular classroom elementary curriculum. Therefore, learning experiences in physical education should be used to reinforce these habits and provide clear associations between wellness and regular physical activity.

Heredity plays a large role in determining a person's physique or body type—people have different body types due to the genetic makeup of their parents and grandparents. The three basic body types or physical classifications are endomorph, mesomorph, and ectomorph (see Figure 3.7 for examples of these classifications). It's important to realize that most people are actually combinations of two of these body types, but everyone is born with a tendency toward a certain basic body type.

Body Composition

Body composition is the amount of fat cells compared to lean cells in the body. Lean body mass is the nonfat tissue composed of muscles, bones, ligaments, and tendons. Fat cells are stored calories

 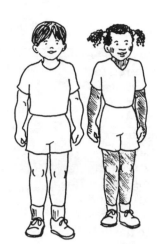 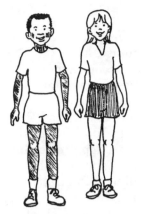

Endomorph—Large body structure; higher percentage of body fat

Mesomorph—Firm, well-developed muscles; broad shoulders

Ectomorph—Small bone structure; slender body characteristics

Figure 3.7 Body types.

that have not been used yet. A certain amount of body fat is essential for good health, but an extremely high or low amount of body fat contributes to health and emotional problems. Obesity refers to the condition of excess body fat (approximately 30% or more fat) that often leads to health problems. Obese people tend to experience more problems with muscles and joints because the extra weight places additional stress on the joints and cardiorespiratory system. Obesity is associated with increased incidence of diabetes. Emotional problems arise from the teasing and ridicule that other children inflict.

Obesity is one of the serious risk factors associated with heart disease. Other risk factors of heart disease that are influenced by the type of lifestyle we lead are smoking, high cholesterol, high blood pressure, extreme stress, and inactivity. These risk factors begin to show up during the childhood years. Therefore, it is important to help children begin to understand these risk factors and develop healthy lifestyles that will reduce them.

We tend to confuse actual body weight with body composition. Lean muscle actually weighs more than the same amount of fat tissue, so a youngster who weighs 100 pounds could be very muscular and physically fit, whereas another student who weighs 100 pounds could be overly fat and unfit. Because exercise and the level of activity play such important roles in maintaining normal body composition, the concept of an active lifestyle is one that should be emphasized in physical education programs.

Caloric Balance

A person's percent of body fat is determined by heredity, eating habits, and the level of physical activity. The balance of calories taken into the body and calories used up in work and play is called the caloric balance equation. Figure 3.8 illustrates the results of various combinations of food intake and activity level.

Body composition is a fitness component that can't be changed in a short period of time. Maintenance of a normal and healthy body weight is best achieved through a combination of healthy eating habits and exercise. Changes in nutritional and activity habits must be carefully planned and incorporated into a daily routine for a long time to change body composition.

Self-Management Strategies

Even when armed with fitness facts and good intentions many children will not participate in physical activity without some behavior management strategies. You can help children examine their own behavior, set goals, and use strategies to follow through and accomplish their goals by using the following strategies:

- Have each child list reasons to be active.
- Have each child choose activities that he or she enjoys.
- Set realistic short-term goals.
- Have children use self-monitoring and graphing activities.
- Have children establish self-rewards.
- Enlist family and friends as social support.
- Use strategies to change the environment and encourage healthy behaviors. For example, ask children to write notes like "be active" or "drink

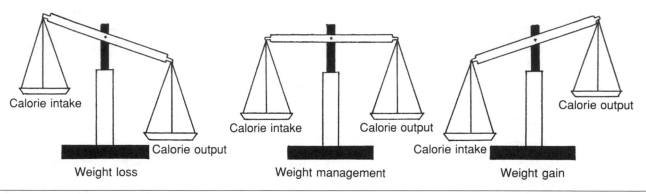

Figure 3.8   Caloric balance equation.

low-fat milk" and to stick these notes where they will see them often—on their books or desks.

- Use self-talk strategies. For example, use positive and motivating phrases like "I can do this!"
- Make specific plans for accomplishing activity goals. Use goal sheets.

An added bonus for children using these strategies is that these self-management techniques are helpful to use when attempting to accomplish all types of goals, not just fitness goals.

Reward systems, including offering material rewards for accomplishing fitness activities, may be necessary and helpful to get some students started on the path to regular exercise habits. Examples of rewards are certificates, ribbons, stickers, buttons, and points toward buying things in the school store. Tangible rewards must be attractive to children, inexpensive, and consistent with the goals of health and fitness. Awarding candy for exercising certainly is not consistent! These extrinsic rewards should be reinforced intermittently and phased out gradually. Motivational support, however, should continue in the form of verbal comments or personal notes to a student concerning healthy fitness habits and attaining goals.

Measuring Body Composition

Measuring body fat in children is accomplished by measuring the thickness of skinfolds because approximately half of the body's fat is located just beneath the skin. A skinfold caliper is used to measure the thickness of a fold of skin and its underlying layer of fat at specific sites on the body (see Figure 3.9). Standards and interpretations of skinfold measurements can be found in the fitness testing programs referenced in chapter 5.

Primary Level Fitness Concepts

For healthy habits and wellness primary students (grades pre-K–2) should be able to

- learn the meaning of healthy habits and
- identify habits that are healthy for the body:
  - getting regular activity—movement and play;
  - eating breakfast and avoiding unhealthy snacks;
  - eating from the food groups pyramid (Figure 3.10);
  - getting adequate rest;
  - maintaining cleanliness and hygiene; and
  - avoiding smoking, drugs, and alcohol.

Intermediate Level Fitness Concepts

For healthy habits and wellness intermediate students (grades 3–6) should be able to

- review primary concepts,
- identify the concept of body composition and how to measure body fat by taking skinfold measurements,

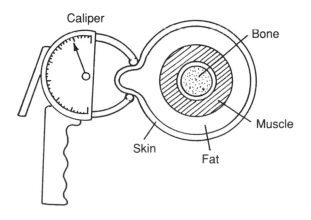

Figure 3.9   Skinfold measurement.

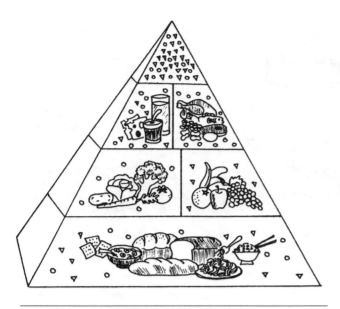

Figure 3.10 Food guide pyramid. *Note.* From the U.S. Department of Agriculture/U.S. Department of Health and Human Services.

- identify the different body types,
- identify the meaning of caloric balance and how to maintain a normal body weight through

proper nutrition (eating wisely from the food groups) and regular exercise, and
- set and accomplish personal fitness goals.

Summary

This chapter has outlined the important fitness concepts that children should learn and experience during their elementary school years. To help you plan your lessons, we have organized fitness information into five categories—introducing fitness concepts, cardiorespiratory endurance, muscular strength and endurance, flexibility, and healthy habits and wellness. We have presented background information and listed important fitness concepts for each category. The fitness concepts have been divided into those most appropriate for pre-kindergarten through second grade (primary level fitness concepts) and those more appropriate for third through sixth grades (intermediate level fitness concepts). In Part II of this book we will present sample learning experiences for each category to illustrate how physical fitness concepts can be taught in school physical education settings.

Chapter 4

Principles for Teaching Fitness

How fitness is taught will have a major impact on children's participation in, understanding of, and feelings about fitness activities and physical activity. If the goal of teaching fitness is to help children develop regular habits of physical activity, knowledge of basic fitness concepts, and positive feelings about physical activity, then the learning experiences must inspire competence and confidence.

Experiences filled with criticism, embarrassment, and monotony will turn children off, whereas experiences filled with success, variety, and personal meaning will motivate many children to adopt a fitness lifestyle. The following guidelines can help you teach developmentally appropriate fitness lessons. They include planning strategies, principles for effective instruction, physical fitness testing, behaviors to avoid, physiological considerations, and a list of harmful exercises and safe alternatives.

Planning Strategies

A variety of strategies is necessary to help students understand and experience the fitness curriculum. One strategy is using a series of lessons on a fitness topic, similar to teaching a sequence of lessons on a motor skill. Another strategy is to incorporate fitness concepts into other lesson themes. For example, flexibility and muscular strength are central to gymnastics. Practicing correct stretches can provide a link between fitness and successful performance of gymnastics skills. The strategy of relating fitness concepts to skill themes is an effective way to reemphasize a concept and provide additional

practice time. On the other hand, if fitness concepts are quickly mentioned and not practiced this strategy can result in students confusing the concept with others or losing it among other lesson ideas. A third strategy is to design out-of-class challenges and activities to help students discover and practice the fitness concepts. The learning experiences found in chapters 6 through 10 will provide some ideas for implementing all of these strategies.

Several factors will guide your decision of which strategy to use. If the fitness concept or activity is a major objective being introduced for the first time, then dedicating whole lessons would be best. If you are reinforcing or reviewing an activity, then incorporating it into other themes is appropriate. With limited time in physical education programs, out-of-class fitness opportunities are a crucial strategy to employ.

Principles for Effective Instruction

We recommend the following guidelines for presenting fitness lessons to children.

1. *Design fitness activities to accommodate students of varying physical characteristics and ability levels.* You can provide opportunities for all children and motivate children to participate fully by applying the strategies recommended by Graham (1992). Provide options for a task or vary its level of difficulty for groups or individuals. For example, if the task is abdominal strength and endurance,

31

then offer a choice of abdominal curls, sit-ups, and sit-ups with a weight. If the purpose is muscular strength and endurance, offer students a choice of 5, 10, or 15 repetitions for modified pull-ups. These strategies are called teaching by invitation and allow children to make choices (Graham, 1992).

Conducting activities by time allows for varying levels of ability. Asking all students to do 20 sit-ups will usually be too hard for some and too easy for others, whereas doing sit-ups for 30 seconds allows students to do as many as they can at their own pace. Having students practice sustained walking and jogging for 10 minutes focuses on aerobic activity for time, not distance, and allows all the students to travel at their own rates and still start and finish at the same time.

A task can be modified for some students by using intratask variation (Graham, 1992). You could have some children do regular sit-ups and others do curl-ups. A situation that invariably occurs during the mile run is an obese child's struggle to finish while everyone waits and watches. This potentially humiliating situation is a time for individual modifications. You could have children engage in another activity in another location as soon as they finish. Or you could arrange to have the obese child run only a half mile or run at another time. Whatever modification you choose, it is important to establish realistic goals for the overweight child. When planning fitness learning experiences, think in terms of organizing a task so *all* students can find some level of success.

2. *Clarify the goals and key points of your fitness lessons.* Use a set induction (Graham, 1992) to present an activity and stimulate interest in it. The tendency in physical education is to do activities and *assume* that students will understand the purpose. Explain to children the purpose of doing the activities! For example, before and after practicing climbing activities such as the horizontal ladder walk and arm hang on the playground bars, assemble the children and ask them questions to help them learn the purpose and benefits of doing the climbing activities.

3. *Review key points during the lesson.* Present one important concept at a time and use a cue to reinforce the concept during the lesson (Graham, 1992). Just as you would refine techniques to improve throwing, you should also observe and refine fitness performance. For example, refinements can help children learn the correct procedures for static stretching, bent-leg sit-ups, pacing for endurance runs, and the position of the fingers for taking the pulse. It is also helpful to use a brief closure after activities or at the end of a lesson to review the key points (Graham, 1992).

4. *Check for understanding by using procedures that encourage all children to think and physically respond (Graham, 1992).* Build in periodic opportunities to check students' understanding by asking them to physically demonstrate, state answers to a partner, or signal the choice between options. For example, have all students show the correct starting position for a sit-up, observe their positions, and give them feedback. Another strategy is to have one student show or tell a partner the correct response. For example, have one partner show the other the size and location of the heart. More examples are provided in chapter 5 in the section about assessment.

5. *Use hands-on experiences to supplement presentations of information.* Use visual aids (Sander & Burton, 1989) and accurate, complete demonstrations to make your key points (see Figure 4.1). Children will understand and remember concepts best by hearing, seeing, and doing.

6. *Repeat learning experiences throughout the year and in subsequent years.* Students will need repeated exposure and repetition to learn fitness information just as they need repeated practice to learn motor skills. Consider the thousands of swings it takes to become proficient at hitting a baseball. It takes many repetitions for children to learn fitness concepts also. Therefore, provide a variety of learning experiences focusing on the same fitness concept.

7. *Provide challenges to encourage regular participation in activities that result in achieving specific goals.* For example, to encourage use of arms and shoulders use the Monkey Bar Club (see p. 86 for details). To encourage regular aerobic activity

Figure 4.1   Teacher using visual aids.

use the Fitness Club (see chapter 7 for details). These clubs offer an opportunity for all students to be successful at their own level of ability and motivation.

8. *Relate fitness concepts to experiences in the children's lives.* For example, improved cardiorespiratory endurance will give them more stamina for playing on the recreational soccer team or playing tag on the playground—they won't have to stop from exhaustion.

Point out the relevance of fitness concepts to different movement themes in the curriculum (see Figure 4.2). Students need help in applying a fitness concept to a new situation. For example, before vigorous soccer activities, review the concept of warm-up by telling students that the purpose of the warm-up is to prepare the muscles for work by increasing blood circulation. Another example is to teach students that the curling movements made during gymnastics class require strong abdominal muscles. Remind students about the curl-ups and sit-ups that they practiced during other class periods. Or you could link the fitness concept of aerobic endurance to successful and enjoyable performance

in games like tag and soccer keep-away. These situations provide excellent teachable moments for clarifying and reviewing fitness information.

9. *Use hands-on learning experiences.* The fitness curriculum should include experiences to help students learn how to do fitness activities and exercises safely and correctly and provide opportunities to achieve a healthy level of fitness in and out of physical education class. The best approach is certainly not to simply stand up and lecture students about fitness. Instead, the key is to provide information through *active, hands-on learning experiences* during physical education classes and then offer challenges and incentives to encourage kids to participate in fitness activities in their daily lives.

Physical Fitness Testing

Fitness testing should be used as part of the ongoing process of educating and challenging students to improve or maintain their physical health and well-being. Formal testing and self-testing should provide opportunities for the teacher and students to

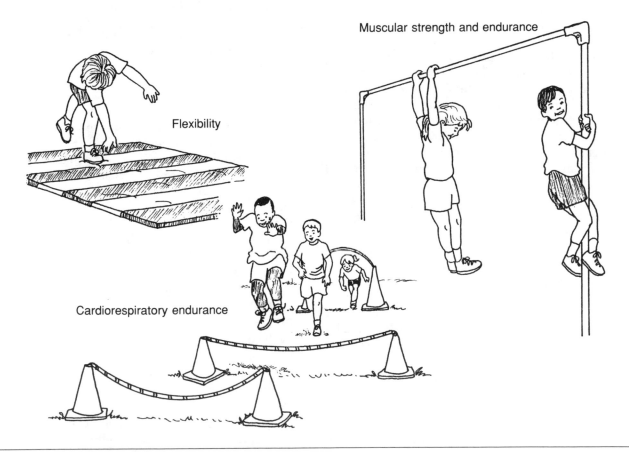

Figure 4.2 Application of fitness concepts.

measure progress and to learn the purpose and importance of the fitness components. It is inappropriate to give fitness tests once or twice a year *solely* for the purpose of qualifying children for awards or because they are required by a school district.

Formal testing makes use of a packaged fitness test (see chapter 5) to collect accurate fitness scores for the following purposes:

- Identifying students who need remedial help on one or more fitness components
- Identifying overall weak areas that need attention; for example, if the average scores on the sit-up test are low, then future lessons can address the need for abdominal activities
- Comparing with criterion scores and norm-referenced scores
- Measuring progress
- Rewarding improvements

Self-testing can be accomplished by students going to a testing station to perform a fitness activity and then comparing their results with a range of scores on a chart. Self-testing could also involve students in cooperating with a partner to test each other on fitness items. Partner testing and self-testing can be valuable strategies to challenge students and to help them learn how to assess themselves.

Children should be physically and emotionally prepared so they can safely complete each component of a physical test battery. It is inappropriate to require children to take fitness tests without adequate conditioning and preparation. You should explain test items and provide practice before you conduct the tests. For example, prior to the mile-run test give children opportunities to run for sustained periods of time. You should also help children understand why they are performing the tests and the meaning of their individual results. We will discuss this further in chapter 5.

Test results shared privately with children and their parents will help develop their physical fitness knowledge and motivate the children to accomplish goals. After conducting a battery of fitness tests, compile individual scorecards for each student. It is helpful to use a large chart and provide an explanation of the scorecard prior to handing out the scores to individuals (see Figure 4.3). A talk about respecting each other's privacy is helpful. Point out to children that some may not want to share their personal scores, just as they may not want to share their grades on their report cards.

If results are sent home to parents the information should interpret the scores and offer some

Figure 4.3 Teacher explaining scorecard.

recommendations. The packaged physical fitness assessment and educational programs listed in chapter 5 provide computer printouts for each student with letters to parents explaining the purpose of the tests, interpreting results, and suggesting activities to improve and maintain individual fitness levels.

Behaviors to Avoid

Certain teaching behaviors can undermine your attempts to motivate children's interest and participation in fitness activities. Try to avoid the following teaching behaviors.

1. *Avoid lecturing as your typical approach to teaching fitness.* Think of ways to get students actively involved in fitness concepts. Some ideas are to use visual aids, stations arranged to describe key facts (see Figure 4.4), task cards, and guided discovery or problem-solving strategies. Also be sure to have all students participate in activities that illustrate the concept. The learning experiences in chapters 6 through 10 are designed to help children learn fitness information by using these strategies.

2. *Avoid using fitness activities as punishment for behavior.* This gives students the message that fitness activities are unpleasant and should be avoided. Instead, offer fitness activities as part of your regular physical education program. Occasionally, offer the opportunity to run or exercise with equipment as a reward to those who complete other tasks.

3. *Avoid making negative comments about a poor performance.* Criticizing or yelling at students to do better will not achieve long-term benefits. If you

Figure 4.4 Lecturing versus active involvement.

see a poor performance, schedule a private discussion with the student and listen to the reasons for it. You can then explain how the student's behavior appeared to you and what you would like to see the next time. This may be enough to motivate the student to exert more effort.

4. *Don't give students the message of "no pain, no gain."* This phrase does not apply to the activities in this book. Children should be taught the difference between initial fatigue, or discomfort, and pain, which may result in injury. Pain is the body's signal to slow down or stop.

Physiological Considerations

Children are *not* miniature adults! You probably have heard this message before, and it applies to fitness as well as motor skills. Although there are many similarities in how children and adults respond to exercise, there are differences in performance. Children's physiological systems are undergoing change in growth and development. For many reasons children cannot perform as efficiently as

adults and should not be compared to adult standards (Rowland, 1990). Children's locomotor performance is less efficient and their smaller and less developed muscular systems limit performance in activities requiring strength and endurance. Lower cardiac output and lower hemoglobin concentrations limit aerobic capacity as compared to adults. Children also are unable to generate anaerobic energy, necessary for short bursts of energy, as efficiently as adults. Hence the following points should be considered when teaching fitness to children.

Although a warm-up period before vigorous exercise is a sound principle, the type of warm-up can and should vary in children's physical education classes. If the same routine is repeated for every class throughout the year, then children will probably become bored and careless when performing the movements, and will fail to see the meaning in the routine. A gentle, whole-body, large-muscle activity should precede any vigorous exercise. A warm-up activity can have many purposes—it prepares the body for exercise by elevating heart rate and increasing circulation to the working muscles, it focuses children's attention, it can be used to practice previously learned skills and behaviors, and it reinforces the message to children that warming up is an important principle of exercise. Be sure to use a warm-up appropriate for your purpose. A throwing lesson could begin with partners gently throwing a ball to each other. A fitness lesson could start with a series of exercises performed to music.

It can be helpful to use an "instant activity" (Graham, 1992) to start a class quickly and serve as a warm-up before the main lesson. As children arrive for class, they should pick up any necessary equipment and begin the activity right away, and not need to assemble to receive instructions. Examples of instant activities include individual jumping rope, individual dribbling practice, partner sit-ups, or a series of low-impact, whole-body calisthenics.

Children will need information about the reactions and feelings they get when involved in vigorous exercise, such as getting out of breath, the burning feeling during strenuous muscle exercise, stitches when running, and sweating. Acknowledging these feelings and responding to the body's messages will help children understand these normal responses and interpret them correctly.

Remember that children have less efficient mechanisms than adults to get rid of body heat. Children's sweat glands put out only about 40% as much sweat as those of adults although children produce more body heat during a given amount of physical activity than adults. Therefore, children have less tolerance for exercise in the heat.

Don't conduct activities in dangerous environmental conditions. Vigorous exercise should not be performed outdoors in excessive heat or humidity or when the air quality is poor. Plan opportunities for children to drink water and ask the classroom teachers to encourage frequent drinking at appropriate times before and after physical education class. Educate students and teachers about the importance of fluid replacement.

Primary age children, pre-kindergarten through second grade, should be encouraged to do exercises that use the resistance of their own body weight, not external weights. Intermediate age prepubescent children can increase their muscle power and strength by systematic weight training but only under the close supervision of an adult who understands correct techniques (Rowland, 1990). Weight training should allow for at least 8 to 10 repetitions rather than a few very heavy lifts. Power lifting with heavy weights should definitely be avoided. An important guideline to use with children is to provide training experience only if the child expresses an interest in it. Imposing adult fitness regimens, such as weight training or running, can result in injury and in diminishing the child's interest in the activity.

Harmful Exercises and Safe Alternatives

Some exercises that have traditionally been taught in physical education classes have the potential to cause injury. A list of exercises that are considered risky and should be avoided follows, along with alternative, safer exercises. This is only a partial list of the most common exercises—you'll find additional information on this topic in Corbin and Lindsey (1991). To maximize safety during exercises be sure children follow these general guidelines:

- Do not hyperextend the knee, neck, or lower back.
- Do not hyperflex the knee or neck.
- Do not hold the breath during exercise.
- Avoid overstretching any joint to the extent that ligaments and joint capsules are stretched.

Harmful Exercises	**Safe Alternatives**

Double Leg Lift

Causes the back to arch and puts pressure on the spine (Figure 4.5).

Reverse Curl

Helps strengthen lower abdominal muscles without excessive stretch on lower back (Figure 4.6). Lift knees to chest, raising hips off the floor, but do not let knees go past the shoulders. Return to starting position, and repeat.

Figure 4.5   Double leg lift.

Figure 4.6   Reverse curl.

**Straight Leg Sit-Up
With Hands Behind the Head**

Causes excessive stress on spine and lower back. Causes pulling and hyperflexion on the neck (Figure 4.7).

Bent Knee Sit-Up

Helps strengthen abdominal muscles. Cross arms on chest with hands on shoulders; tighten up abdominal muscles and rise up to touch elbows to thighs. Then return to starting position and repeat (Figure 4.8).

Figure 4.7   Straight leg sit-up with hands behind the neck.

Figure 4.8   Bent knee sit-up.

Curl-Ups

Helps strengthen abdominal muscles. Use fingers on side of head to support neck; tighten up abdominal muscles; lift shoulders and hold for 6 or more seconds; then relax to starting position (Figure 4.9).

Figure 4.9   Curl-ups.

Harmful Exercises	Safe Alternatives

Deep Knee Bend
Causes hyperflexion, stretching, and stress to the knee joint (Figure 4.10).

Forward Lunge
To stretch the quadricep, hip, and thigh muscles, take a step forward with the right foot, touching left knee to floor. Knees should be bent no further than 90 degrees. Repeat with the other foot (Figure 4.11).

Figure 4.10   Deep knee bend.

Figure 4.11   Forward lunge.

Standing Toe Touch With Straight Legs
Causes stretching of the ligaments and joint capsule of the knee (Figure 4.12).

Toe Touch With Slightly Bent Knees
This stretches the hamstring muscles and avoids straining the knee ligaments (Figure 4.13).

Figure 4.12   Standing toe touch.

Figure 4.13   Bent-knee toe touch.

Neck Circles
Tipping the head backward during any exercise can pinch arteries and nerves in the neck and put pressure on the discs (Figure 4.14).

Neck Stretch
Instead of tipping the head back, stretch the neck muscles by dropping the head forward and slowly moving it in a half circle to the right and then left (Figure 4.15).

Figure 4.14   Neck circles.

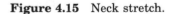

Figure 4.15   Neck stretch.

Harmful Exercises	**Safe Alternatives**

Donkey Kick

Hyperextension and arching of lower back results when foot position is higher than the buttocks (Figure 4.16).

Knee-to-Nose Touch

To strengthen the buttocks muscles, keep the back straight with the leg in line with the back; keep head straight and in line with back; focus eyes at floor (Figure 4.17).

Figure 4.16   Donkey kick.

Figure 4.17   Knee-to-nose touch.

Ballistic Bar Stretch

Potentially harmful to the knee joint when extended leg is raised 90 degrees or more and trunk is bent over leg (Figure 4.18).

Back-Saver Toe Touch

To stretch the hamstrings, sit with one foot against the wall or extended out with one knee bent. Clasp hands behind the back and bend forward, keeping lower back as straight as possible (Figure 4.19).

Figure 4.18   Ballistic bar stretch.

Figure 4.19   Back-saver toe touch.

Hurdler's Stretch

Puts the knee in a rotated position, which can cause excess stretching of the ligaments and damage to the cartilage (Figure 4.20).

Hamstring Stretch

To stretch the hamstring and calf muscles, lie on the back with knees bent. Raise one leg and grasp toes while pulling on back of thigh. Push heel toward ceiling and hold. Repeat with other leg (Figure 4.21).

Figure 4.20   Hurdler's stretch.

Figure 4.21   Hamstring stretch.

Summary

The fitness experiences provided for children can have an immediate and lasting effect on their attitudes and future participation in physical activity. The principles provided in this chapter are intended to help children learn specific, meaningful information about fitness in an enjoyable environment. These guidelines should help prevent fitness experiences that result in embarrassment and failure, repetitious exercises that lack purpose, and fitness testing that fails to help children set and achieve personal goals.

This chapter has described some of the specific instructional strategies teachers can use to plan and implement successful fitness lessons. Sections of this chapter discussed aspects to consider when using fitness tests, behaviors to avoid when teaching fitness concepts, physiological considerations applicable to children, and some exercises to avoid along with safer alternatives.

Chapter 5

Assessing Children's Progress in Fitness

Earlier we stated that our goals for teaching fitness were to help children achieve a healthy level of physical fitness, increase their regular participation in fitness activities, learn concepts associated with physical fitness, and develop positive attitudes about exercise.

Chapters 6 through 10 provide sample learning experiences that can be used to achieve these goals. This chapter will describe procedures to assess how well they accomplish these goals.

Assessing the Psychomotor Domain

Fitness testing is by far the most common type of assessment used in physical education classes. Fitness testing should assess each student's current level of fitness, assist each student in setting personal fitness goals, guide the planning and evaluation of the fitness education curriculum, and educate students about fitness concepts. Done correctly, the process of fitness testing will teach students the components of fitness, how to measure each component, and what to do to improve their fitness scores.

A number of nationally recognized health-related physical fitness assessment programs are presently available. Although these programs are periodically revised, the most commonly used testing packages are these:

Physical Best Fitness Assessment and Education Program
American Alliance for Health, Physical Education, Recreation and Dance
1900 Association Dr.
Reston, VA 22091
703-476-3455 or 800-321-0789

FITNESSGRAM
Institute for Aerobics Research
12330 Preston Rd.
Dallas, TX 75230
800-635-7050
(Sponsored by Prudential Insurance)

Chrysler Fund—AAU Physical Fitness Program
Poplars Building
Indiana University
Bloomington, IN 47405
800-258-5497
(Sponsored by the Chrysler Corporation Fund)

President's Challenge Physical Fitness Program
President's Council on Physical Fitness and Sports
450 5th Street, N.W., Ste. 7103
Washington, DC 20001
800-258-8146

Regardless of which testing program you use, the following guidelines will help you establish an appropriate testing environment and administer the tests efficiently.

Before administering a fitness test you should prepare by reviewing the test manual and practicing the specific procedures for each test item. You should also review the medical status of your students and identify those children with asthma or other conditions so they can be properly prepared for taking the tests. For example, contact parents of asthmatic children to be sure that medication is used before the endurance run, and consider possible test modifications for obese children and discuss these choices with them. You'll then need to develop a testing schedule, train your assistants, and prepare your students for testing by conducting orientation and practice sessions.

Testing Administration

You can choose from several successful methods for administering the tests. In the station method the class is divided into several groups and each group is assigned to a different activity or station. One station tests a fitness component, allowing a small group of students to take the test while other groups participate in activities that do not require direct supervision. This procedure allows the teacher to concentrate on a small group, but it requires that other children in the class cooperate independently at their activities. After the test is completed the students rotate to the next station. If assistants are available more than one station can be used for testing.

The pull-out method is similar to the station method except that all the students are involved in the same activity and the teacher calls out students to be tested. Again this procedure allows the teacher to focus attention on testing a small number of students at a time, but it requires that students are able to cooperate independently. These methods for organizing testing eliminate long lines, which result in wasted time, and minimize the potential for embarrassment when students watch others be tested.

Administering a battery of fitness tests by yourself is time-consuming and difficult. Try to recruit parents, classroom teachers, high school or university students, or other community members to help with the testing. After some initial planning and training, these volunteers can help you conduct the tests quickly and accurately.

Individual and partner self-testing is a method that places responsibility on students for conducting their own tests. Stations are set up with the necessary equipment, and students in partners are taught how to conduct the tests and record results for each other. This method sacrifices teacher con-

trol over the accuracy of the results, but gives students more investment in their own scores and helps them learn how to conduct the tests. At first this method may not work very well with students who are accustomed to teacher testing, but over time students can learn to test themselves and others more honestly without fear of being graded, criticized, or compared with others.

If the purpose for the tests is to get accurate results, then teacher control of the testing environment is necessary, but if the purpose is to help children learn how to measure various aspects of fitness and evaluate their own progress toward fitness goals, then self-testing has important benefits.

Scheduling

Many factors will affect your scheduling of fitness tests, including class size, length of class periods, facilities, assistance, experience of the students, and your purpose. All components of fitness can be tested during one block of time (consecutive day plan) or one component can be tested at a time as children learn and participate in related activities (periodic plan).

The consecutive day plan means that a test is given during each lesson during four or five consecutive class meetings until all tests are completed. A periodic plan means that the tests are given at different times during the school year and can coincide with other topics in the curriculum. For instance the sit-and-reach test could be administered as part of a series of lessons on flexibility, or flexibility information including a sit-and-reach test could be included as part of a gymnastics unit.

Interpreting Test Results

Formal fitness testing can provide useful information concerning the fitness levels of your students, but the results must be interpreted in light of natural ability, maturation, and motivation. Some children who don't participate in regular exercise can score well on the tests just because they are genetically endowed. Children's scores may decrease because of growth spurts that add bone and tissue weight ahead of muscular development. Motivation and effort during the tests will make a major difference in the final scores. For these reasons and because scoring procedures are susceptible to error, the results of fitness tests have to be examined and used carefully.

Assessing Activity Outside of Class

If our main objective is to encourage children to participate in regular physical activity, then other assessments besides fitness testing can be very revealing. A convenient method of assessment is to document students' participation in physical activity outside of class. If you are conducting a Fitness Club (see chapter 7) you can tally the number of children and extent of participation by inspecting their recording charts. Another strategy to encourage and document children's participation in regular physical activity outside of school is a Home Exercise Program. Participants earn points when their parents sign a form similar to the one in Figure 5.1 to verify that they completed an activity. Points for the activities are credited toward an individual or class reward. A helpful strategy to involve parents and children is to reward bonus points if a parent exercises or participates with the child.

Assessing the Cognitive Domain

A major objective of teaching fitness is to help children understand the basic concepts of physical fitness. Cognitive learning can be assessed through the use of worksheets, knowledge tests, homework assignments, and checks for understanding.

Worksheets

Worksheets are used to review information and reinforce children's learning. They must be designed to match the information you are teaching, and they must be appropriate for the children's cognitive developmental level. A helpful procedure is to check the appropriateness of your worksheets with the classroom teacher. For example, the Heart Pump and Blood Flow worksheet in chapter 7 is designed to review and reinforce information children learned in the heart and circulatory system obstacle course. Organizations such as the American Heart Association provide this and other worksheets.

Written Tests

Paper and pencil knowledge tests can help measure children's cognitive understanding of fitness concepts. Design tests to match the children's cognitive level and to reflect what is being taught in the fitness lessons. Multiple choice, true-false, fill-in-the-blanks, matching, open-ended tests, or combinations of all these tests are useful to assess children's knowledge. Examples of these types of tests are shown in Figures 5.2 and 5.3.

Good questions take time to write and often need to be revised based on children's responses and levels of understanding. In time, however, a battery of questions can be developed that reflect what children should be learning in physical fitness lessons. Some excellent test materials for different age groups are available from the American Heart Association.

We acknowledge that testing children in physical education classes is difficult and controversial. Large numbers of students, limited contact time,

My child did the following physical activity to develop his or her physical fitness. (Write the activities in the spaces below.)

_____

_____

_____

_____

Extra credit is awarded for activities done with a parent. (Detail such activities below.)

_____

_____

_____   _____
Parent signature   Date

Return to your physical education teacher.

Figure 5.1 Home exercise recording form.

Multiple Choice: Circle all the correct answers. You can have more than one correct answer for each question.

1. Good physical fitness means
    a. being able to run and play during recess without getting tired
    b. watching TV
    c. being able to run and walk for long distances
    d. being able to play computer games without getting tired

2. A muscle will get stronger if you
    a. rest it a little bit
    b. give it lots of extra rest
    c. eat more food
    d. overload it
    e. I don't know

3. Sit-ups help strengthen the
    a. arm and shoulder muscles
    b. leg muscles
    c. abdominal muscles
    d. heart
    e. I don't know

True-False

1. You should exercise once a week to be fit and healthy.   True   False
2. The heart is a muscle that pumps blood.   True   False

Matching: Match the fitness words with the best exercise:

flexibility	cartwheels and handstands
arm strength/endurance	stretching exercises
aerobic endurance	running sprints
speed	distance running

Figure 5.2   Sample physical fitness test questions.

and activity environments not suited to paper and pencil tests present problems to consider. To help alleviate these problems, test various classes and grades at different times, ask only a few key questions at a time, find assistants to score the tests, use clipboards to organize the papers, and have your classroom teachers administer the tests.

Homework Assignments

Another effective way to alleviate the time and administrative restraints in your physical education classes is to assign worksheets and projects as homework. Have students make posters using their own drawings or magazine photographs on the following topics: activities that keep you "in shape" or fit, risk factors of heart disease and how to reduce them, and components of health-related and skill-related fitness. Topics for written reports include

how to get "in shape" or fit and why regular activity is important. Another idea is to have children keep a log of their exercise and physical activities. All these projects work best when coordinated with the classroom teachers and parents to provide support for children's efforts.

Checking for Understanding

To assess children's understanding of fitness concepts during instruction you can use a technique called checking for understanding (Graham, 1992). This technique requires children to verbally or physically demonstrate their understanding. For example, have students show the correct position for the sit-up or show an exercise that helps make the arms and shoulders stronger. You can walk around to make sure they all demonstrate the correct position. Physically showing the answer will

1. Write in the two types of physical fitness. Give an example of each.

    a. _____   Example_____

    b. _____   Example_____

2. Write three benefits of regular physical activity.

    a. _____

    b. _____

    c. _____

3. Write in the physical fitness test that measures your performance in each fitness component.

    Cardiorespiratory endurance   _____

    Muscular strength and endurance   _____

    Flexibility   _____

    Body composition   _____

Open-Ended Question

   Your friend Murgatroid would like to get in shape to improve the cardiorespiratory system, but
   does not know what activities to do. List three physical fitness activities that Murgatroid could
   do to improve cardiorespiratory endurance.

Figure 5.3   Sample fill-in-the-blanks and open-ended test questions.

allow all children to be involved and help you identify those children who don't understand so you can assist them.

Another strategy for checking for understanding is to have all students give a visual response to a question so they have to think about the question and decide on an answer. For example, as part of a closure to an aerobic endurance lesson, ask students to respond to the statement "Walking for a couple of minutes is a good way to improve your aerobic endurance." If they think the statement is true they should show a thumbs-up signal, if false, a thumbs-down signal, and if they are unsure they should show a flat-hand, palm-down signal. The teacher can see how all children respond, call on someone to explain the response, and add additional information if necessary. Procedures that cause students to think about options and make a decision will stimulate more thought and help the teacher to see what choices the children are making.

Poker Chip Survey

A procedure used to evaluate cognitive understanding at the end of a class is to have children place a poker chip, straw, popsicle stick, or other object in a container as they go back to class. Make a statement such as "The mile run test is used to measure the flexibility of our muscles and joints" or "Aerobic exercise means lifting weights to build strong muscles." Then ask children to put their chip in the can marked with "yes" if they agree with the statement or in the can marked "no" if they disagree. A quick look at the number of chips in the containers will give you an idea of how well the students understood the concept of the day's lesson.

Assessing the Affective Domain

Another important goal of elementary physical education is to help children develop a positive attitude about exercise and enjoy participating in regular physical activities. Children will usually express their feelings so you will get a general idea of how much they enjoy coming to physical education and participating in the activities. On the other hand, you may get the views of some vocal children and not those of more reticent students. Therefore, it may be useful to collect information from all the children about how they feel toward physical education class, physical activity, and their abilities.

Smiley-Face Exit Poll

A simple way to find out how children feel is to survey them by asking them to give a thumbs-up signal if they enjoyed the class and felt good about participating in it, a thumbs-down signal if they did not enjoy it or feel good about it, and a flat-hand, palm-down sign if it was just okay. A more formal procedure is to use a smiley-face exit poll similar to the poker chip survey (Graham, 1992). Children can choose a laminated smiley, neutral, or frowny face as they leave the class and deposit it in the ballot box. Possible questions to ask them to respond to with the symbols are: How do you feel about your ability to do today's fitness tests? How do you feel about running the mile? How do you feel about doing exercises to music? and How do you feel about today's lesson?

Smiley-Face Questionnaire

Children's attitudes about fitness activities can also be assessed by using paper and pencil smiley-face forms. A sample questionnaire is shown in Figure 5.4. This questionnaire may be administered by the classroom teacher at a convenient time of the day.

Logs, journals, and discussion circles also provide valuable insights into how and what children are learning and thinking about in physical education class. Refer to chapter 12 in *Teaching Children*

1. How do you feel about taking fitness tests?
   (sit-ups, sit-and-reach, pull-ups, running)

2. How do you feel about running and walking for exercise?

3. How do you feel about your physical education class?

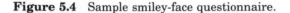

Figure 5.4 Sample smiley-face questionnaire.

Physical Education (Graham, 1992) for more information on using these techniques.

Grading

Many of the procedures presented in this chapter are for the benefit of the teacher to evaluate the effectiveness of the program, to guide future instruction, and to use as support and justification of the program. Some of these procedures can also be used in assigning grades, but simply reporting a letter grade or a satisfactory/unsatisfactory grade is not very helpful for parents. A better system for reporting children's progress to parents is to periodically send home reports that explain what children are learning and information about how the child is doing. Reporting fitness results can be beneficial if the purpose of the tests and the results are explained and if practical suggestions for improvement are included. The national fitness testing programs cited in this chapter have computer programs that print out this information (Figure 5.5). Remember that fitness test results are only one aspect of a total physical education program. If this is the only information sent to parents then it fails to give them a complete view of the goals of your overall program.

Summary

This chapter has presented more examples of ways to assess children's progress in the motor, cognitive, and affective domains than any teacher would use in a single year. It is important to choose testing procedures from among the many available with a specific purpose in mind and then develop them to suit the particular context of your situation. Assessment is an important part of effective teaching. A well thought-out and planned assessment program can provide a barometer of the progress children are making toward achieving the physical, cognitive, and affective fitness goals as well as information to share with parents, school board members, and administrators. In this era of accountability, an assessment program provides an important way to demonstrate the value of our physical education programs for children.

FITNESSGRAM®

Name:	Consuelo Ratliffe	Grade:	6	Section:	H
School:	Wildwood	Instructor:	O'Brien		

Sit-and-reach		Sit-up		Skinfold or body mass index (BMI)			Walk/run		
Centimeters	% rank	Number	% rank	① Skinfold (mm)	BMI (kg/m²)	%Rank	Min:sec or yards	% rank	② Type
33	70	44	80	33	84.4	95	11:10	25	1 mi

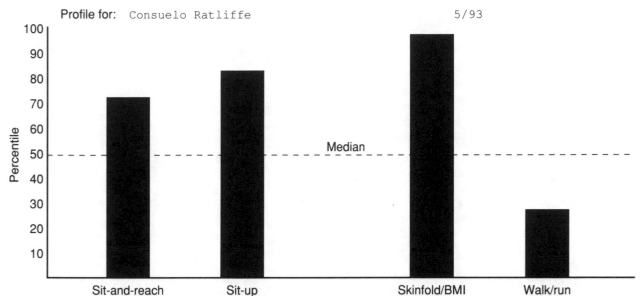

Profile for: Consuelo Ratliffe   5/93

(Bar chart — Percentile on y-axis: Sit-and-reach ≈73, Sit-up ≈83, Skinfold/BMI ≈98, Walk/run ≈28. Median dashed line at 50.)

Total physical fitness score

Excellent . . . . 234+
Above average 211-233
Average 191-210
Below average 167-190
Well below average 0-166

Date	Height	Weight	Total fitness score
mo-yr	ft-in	lbs	
5-93	5-00	99	239

These activities
are recommended:

To improve your cardio-
respiratory endurance: walking,
jogging, swimming, cycling,
and rope jumping.

Dear Parent:

We are pleased to send you this FITNESSGRAM® to provide information on your child's level of physical fitness as indicated by his/her performance in the AAHPERD Health Related Physical Fitness Test recently administered in our school. This test was developed by the American Alliance for Health, Physical Education, Recreation and Dance.

Your child participates in the test at least once a year. The FITNESSGRAM® will show you any progress in his/her growth and development over the school years.

The FITNESSGRAM® provides the following information:

1. A total physical fitness score for your child based on assessments of
   • low-back hamstring flexibility—measured by sit-and-reach test;
   • abdominal strength and endurance—1 minute sit-up test;
   • body composition — indicated by one of the following tests:
     a) measurement of triceps skinfold (back of upper arm) plus subscapular (below shoulder blade) or triceps skinfold only
     b) ratio of weight to height as indicated by Body Mass Index (weight in kilograms divided by height in meters squared)
        Please note, it is not recommended that children already in the 90th percentile attempt to lose more weight;
   • cardiovascular fitness—1-mile, 1.5-mile, 9-minute, or 12-minute walk/run.
2. A percentile rank (% RANK) for each test item is computed based on a norm developed for your child's age and sex. You can see both your child's score and the average (50%) of other students who have taken this test.
3. An exciting feature of the FITNESSGRAM® is the recommendation for activities which can help improve your child's individual scores.
4. The FITNESSGRAM® reflects past performances which will allow the monitoring of improvement from test date to test date within the school year!

We hope you will find the FITNESSGRAM® a useful tool to assess your child's fitness level, height and weight development—and to encourage your entire family to enjoy the benefits of an active lifestyle.

Christine Anderson
Physical Education Instructor

Figure 5.5   Sample fitness report to parents. *Note.* FITNESSGRAM is developed by the Cooper Institute for Aerobics Research, Dallas, Texas, and is sponsored by Prudential Insurance.

Part II

Teaching Developmentally Appropriate Learning Experiences in Fitness

The second part of the book includes five chapters that describe in detail how the content might be developed for teaching children. Each chapter consists of a number of learning experiences (LEs) from which lessons can be developed. From each LE, for example, you might be able to develop two or more lessons, depending on your teaching situation. It is important to realize, however, that in many instances if one were to teach an entire LE as a lesson, the children would no doubt finish confused—and probably frustrated—because LEs contain far more than can be reasonably taught, and learned, in one 30-minute experience. Most LEs contain several objectives. For most lessons you will want to select one, maybe two, objectives to concentrate on. In other words, you want to pick a "learnable piece" that children can truly understand and grasp—rather than simply exposing them to ideas that can't be understood, let alone learned, in the time allotted.

The learning experiences in Part II are organized according to a similar format. This format is as follows:

- The *Name* of the learning experience
- *Objectives* that explain the psychomotor, cognitive, and affective skills children will improve as a result of participating in this learning experience. When appropriate, the NASPE benchmarks that these objectives are helping students meet are referenced in parentheses at the end of an objective. The first character refers to the grade level the benchmark is found under in the official NASPE document, and the second gives the number of the benchmark itself.
- A *Suggested Grade Range* for the learning experience
- The *Organization* that children will be working in during the learning experience
- The kinds and amounts of *Equipment Needed* for presenting this learning experience to children
- A *Description* of the total learning experience, explained as if the physical education teacher was actually presenting the learning experience to children (additional information for teachers is set off in brackets)
- *Look For*, which gives key points for teachers to keep in mind when informally observing children's progress in the learning experience. These are related to the objectives for the LE.
- *How Can I Change This?*, which allows you to either increase or decrease the difficulty level involved in the learning experience, thus allowing for all students to be challenged at their ability levels

- *Teachable Moments*, those perfect opportunities either during or after a lesson to discuss how a cognitive or affective concept is related to what has occurred in the learning experience

The next five chapters describe specific learning experiences for the following fitness categories:

- introducing fitness concepts (chapter 6)
- cardiorespiratory endurance (chapter 7)
- muscular strength and endurance (chapter 8)
- flexibility (chapter 9)
- healthy habits and wellness (chapter 10)

We have described a limited number of learning experiences in detail, rather than listing a series of activities. This approach is intended to provide you with enough information to understand how the fitness concepts are taught to children by blending verbal instruction with activity. These learning experiences have been used successfully in a variety of teaching environments. The References, Suggested Readings, and Additional Resources at the end of the book will provide other ideas and help you develop your own learning experiences.

Chapter 6

Learning Experiences for Introducing Fitness Concepts

The learning experiences in this chapter are intended to help children develop an understanding of the meaning of physical fitness, the types and components of fitness, the personal health benefits of being fit, and the principles used to develop fitness. These basics will provide a foundation for more specific learning experiences that children will begin to participate in during the elementary school years.

These learning experiences provide sample ideas for introducing children to physical fitness concepts. The following list of the focus and suggested grade range of the learning experiences included in this chapter will help you choose appropriate activities for your classes.

Focus	Name	Suggested grade range
"Active" activities	Being Active!	K–2
Benefits of being active	Activity Benefits	Pre-K–2
Defining *good shape*	Shape Up	3–6
Components of health-related fitness	Health-Related Circuit	3–6
The terms *overload, repetition*, and *set*	Making Stronger Muscles	3–6

BEING ACTIVE!

Objectives

As a result of participating in this learning experience, children will improve their ability to

- participate in movement tasks that promote being active (K, #16)
- associate being active with doing healthy heart and large muscle group exercises and activities (K, #20)
- identify different activities that are active and help us to be in good shape

Suggested Grade Range

Primary (Pre-K–2)

Organization

Set up the two activity areas before class. Mark one rectangular cement area for the stations with cones around the perimeter and set up an obstacle course in the other area, preferably on grass. See Figure 6.1 for details.

Equipment Needed

For stations: 6 cards on which one number, 1 through 6, is marked; tape; 4 to 6 basketballs, hula hoops, and objects for the throwing and catching stations (e.g., yarn balls, junior footballs, frisbees, scoops); hoops to hold the objects; a box target for shooting (see Figure 6.2); a record/tape/CD player, and lively, popular music with a strong beat.

For obstacle course: 20 large rubber cones with a hole in top, 4 boxes or milk crates, 8 hoops, 11 spot markers or carpet squares, 2 open-ended hoops, 8 jump ropes, a drum, and 2 posters—1 of people doing inactive activities and 1 of people doing active activities.

Description

"You've heard teachers, your parents, and coaches say that it's important to be in good shape. In today's lesson we want to think about how you can get into good shape. During the lesson ask yourself what you are doing to help your body get into shape. We're going to be doing lots of fun things, so the answers should be easy!

"For the first thing we'll do today, you'll notice that I have six stations set up around the outside of our blacktop area. The number taped to the cone tells you what number each station is. First, I want Mark to run quickly over to the first station. See the basketballs nicely arranged in the hoops? At this station, you'll be dribbling, or bouncing and catching, the ball all kinds of ways in your self-space. The next one is the second station; see where Mark is? Here, you are going to get to move the hula hoop any way you want to. Then, you go to the third station. Here, you get to throw and catch any of the balls to yourself or a partner. At the fourth station, you get to dribble and shoot the basketballs to the box target. Fifth, you get to run around the blacktop area; and last, you get to throw the Frisbees. Come on back, Mark. Did you notice that the equipment was nicely put inside a hoop at each station? I'll expect you to get it and put it back nicely before you switch stations.

"We will be doing our stations to music today. When you are at a station and the music is on, that's the signal to go. When the music stops, what do you think you do?

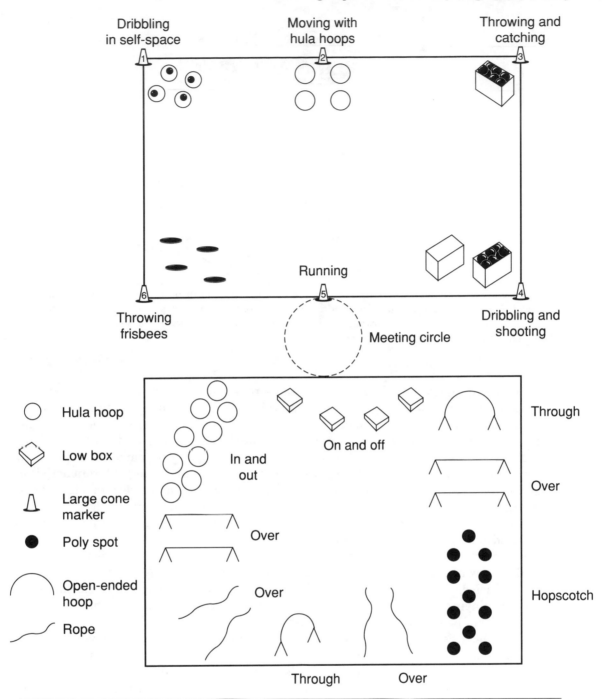

Figure 6.1 Diagram of activity areas.

Yes, you stop. You then will point to the next station you're going to move to, and when the music begins, you can move and begin being active at the next station. Do you think you can remember all that? Any questions? OK, when I tap you on the head I want you to quickly stand up and go to the station number I say, and wait for the music to begin. [Tap and number students so they are equally divided between the stations. When all are assembled, begin music. Give approximately 1 to 3 minutes per station, depending on amount of time available. Make sure students wait and point to the next station before you begin music again. When all have been to each station once . . .] OK, everyone come on over to the meeting circle. Here's a question—what do you think it means to be in good shape? Yes, Drake, it means to have a strong body. Yes, also strong muscles . . . and if you're healthy you get some exercise every day.

Cut flaps from upper edges

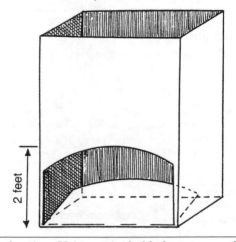

2 feet

Figure 6.2   Box target for shooting. Using a single-blade razor or other cutter, cut an empty refrigerator box along the dashed lines indicated. Put box in desired target location, weighting it down by putting a tire in the bottom. Push the cut flap to the inside of the box, over the tire. Balls shot inside the box should come out this ramp.

Being active gives you a healthy heart and strong muscles. Eating healthy foods also helps keep you in good shape. These are all things that people in good shape do or have.

"Today we are going to *be active*. What did you do already today to be active or keep in shape? Kelly played at recess, Alyssa ate a healthy breakfast, and Brett dribbled a ball. Yes, those are some good answers. Now we are going to learn more about the words *active* and *inactive*. *Active* means the body is moving and doing different activities so lots of energy is used. Inactive means the body doesn't move very much and less energy is used. Everyday we will do some of both types of activities.

"What are some inactive things we do each day? Yes, you're right, Tonya, watching TV and reading. Yes, Rob, playing a quiet game and drawing a picture are inactive types of activities. [Show a poster of people doing inactive activities.] These can be fun and worthwhile, but remember that you need to be active also! Name some ways to be active each day. Good! You've got the idea—playing at recess, doing a physical education lesson, playing tag and sports, dance and gymnastics, and riding a bike are good examples of being active! [Show a poster of people doing active things.]

"Now let's be active again and help our bodies to get into good shape! There are obstacles set up today for you to travel over and under. Jane will demonstrate how to travel through the obstacle course [student demonstration]. Watch her as she jumps over the rope hurdles, then jumps and hops on the poly spots, then jumps over the river [two ropes], goes through the hoop tunnel, over another river, over more hurdles, in and out of the hula hoops, on and off the boxes, through another hoop tunnel, and continues going around again. It's important to keep moving and don't bunch up or stand in line. [If a line develops at one obstacle, take several children from the line to another obstacle on the opposite side of the circuit.] When I call your name, I'll send you to a place on the course where you can begin. [Call on children and send to different parts of the obstacle course to prevent bunching up; allow for 5 to 10 minutes of activity.] Ready, stop and come to the meeting area.

"In today's lesson we talked about how to get our bodies in good shape. What should we do every day to help us be in good shape? That's right, *be active*. What did we do today in physical education that was active? Yes, we dribbled a ball, hula-hooped, and traveled through the obstacle course. Remember, the key to being in good shape is to *be active*. We'll talk a lot more about this during the year."

Look For

- Do children clearly understand why activities are active or inactive? Can children identify numerous examples?
- Observe children during the activity segment of the lesson. Are they continuously moving?

How Can I Change This?

- Set up two obstacle courses for large classes. Use skill themes like soccer dribbling, tag games, or dribbling with the hands as an initial activity instead of the station activities.
- Use the homework assignment in Figure 6.3.

Name: _____   Classroom teacher: _____

Dear Parents:

Your child has been learning about the importance of physical fitness and why it is important to *be active* for good health. Please help your child fill out this assignment and return to his or her physical education teacher.

To be in good shape *B* ___   *A* ___ ___ ___ ___ ___ every day!

Name the different ways of being active in the pictures.

What other ways to be active can you think of? Draw your own pictures of people being active.

Figure 6.3   Be Active homework assignment.

TEACHABLE MOMENT

Make the association between active skill practice and staying in shape. Ask questions that focus on the lesson objectives. For example, "While we were practicing our skills and having fun, did we exercise our hearts? How do you know? (We were breathing harder and our hearts were beating faster than normal.) What other muscles did we use? This afternoon when you leave school, what will you do to be active?"

ACTIVITY BENEFITS

Objectives

As a result of participating in this learning experience, children will improve their ability to

- experience being active by participating in a variety of activities (K, #17)
- realize that the term *active* means to move the body in a variety of activities using lots of energy (1-2, #25)
- identify the benefits of being active

Suggested Grade Range

Primary (Pre-K–2)

Organization

Using marking cones, set up two activity areas before class: Each should be the space of half a basketball court. Spread out balls for half the class and ropes for the other half. Make an "active" poster (see Figure 6.4).

Equipment Needed

14 marking cones, boundary cones, "active" poster (Figure 6.4), jump ropes for half the class, balls for half the class

Description

Take one or two sessions for this lesson, depending on the students' experience with fitness concepts. Use skill activities that have been taught before. Otherwise, you'll spend most of the time on skill development and management, rather than building the connection between being active and physical fitness. "Quickly come over to our meeting circle and sit down. In today's lesson we are going to continue to practice our

Figure 6.4   Sample "active" poster.

jumping skills and bouncing and catching skills. While you practice the skills, think about how these skills help you to *be active*. Remember how we talked last week about being active and what it means?

"Those of you on this side of the circle go to the dribbling activity and begin to dribble and travel in the space inside the boundaries. Now, all of you on this side go to the jump rope area, find a rope, and begin. I see Erica has already started. That's the way to be active! [Encourage children to be active and praise their efforts. After about 5 minutes switch groups. After about 5 minutes more stop the activities and call children to the meeting circle.]

"In our last lesson we learned that to be in good shape we need to be active. Who remembers what *active* means? Yes, Tom, active means to move the body and do different activities like playing, sports, and exercises. The benefits of being active include having a healthy heart and body, feeling good, having more energy, and being able to do more active things. Did you notice that the word *active* is part of the word *activities*?

"What have we done that was active in our lesson? Right, we jumped rope and dribbled. Did doing these activities use more energy than working at your table or watching TV? How do you know? [Make sure students understand that the heart beats faster, they sweat, and breathing increases.]

"Now let's do something else active. We'll practice the pacing game. In this game you jog at a steady pace for as long as you can and continue to walk when you need to. You should try to jog along with the others in the group, but if you get tired, do a brisk exercise walk. No passing is allowed if the person in front of you is jogging. If the person in front of you is walking, then you can jog around them. Who would like to lead today? OK, Keith, today we will practice pacing for 5 minutes. Off you go . . . we'll be following! [The time for this activity varies depending on your purpose—allow 3 to 5 minutes for a warm-up, 5 to 10 minutes for pacing practice, and 15 or more minutes to develop aerobic endurance. After desired practice . . .] Everyone walk back to our meeting circle and begin to do your stretching exercises. [As they stretch] Was the pacing game active? Why? Yes, because we were moving—good, Shonda! When we are active our bodies benefit. What are the good things that being active does for the body? This poster [Figure 6.4] lists some of the benefits for you. Have you enjoyed being active? Well, this is an important benefit, too. Being active not only helps you to have a healthy heart and body and feel good, but being active is fun! When you go home today, try to be active by doing something fun!"

Look For

- Do children understand why certain activities are active and some are not active?
- Can they identify the benefits of being active?

How Can I Change This?

- Substitute different activities for dribbling, jumping rope, and pacing, but be certain that your activities meet the criteria for "Being Active"—sweating, increased rate of breathing, and increased heart rate.
- Use practice centers with directions written out on a chart. Order tasks from simple to complex for the selected skill. Have children progress through the tasks at their own rate.
- Have older children keep a physical fitness journal. After introducing and discussing information about fitness have them write their reflections about what they learned in the lesson.
- Have groups work cooperatively to create a poster that shows ways of being active at school and at home and identifies the benefits of being active.

TEACHABLE MOMENT

In subsequent lessons after children have been involved in any continuous activity, stop and ask if the activity is active. Then ask why—can the children name three or four reasons (heart rate increases, breathing increases, sweating occurs, and large-muscle groups are used)? The message of being active for positive benefits should be reinforced in subsequent classes and periodically throughout the year.

SHAPE UP

Objectives

As a result of participating in this learning experience, children will improve their ability to

- describe characteristics of someone who is in "good shape"
- distinguish between active and inactive behavior patterns (5-6, #18)
- identify ways to be active during school, after school, and at home (5-6, #20)

Suggested Grade Range

Intermediate (3–6)

Organization

Meet in the classroom or suitable place where students can write, where you have a chalkboard or chart paper, and where you can post information. Place children in small groups using established classroom groups if they have them because they will be used to working with each other. Distribute paper and pencils before beginning the class.

Equipment Needed

Paper and pencils for each student, chalkboard or chart paper, chalk or markers

Description

"In physical education we try to help boys and girls learn about moving their bodies in interesting and skillful ways and about taking care of their bodies so that they can grow and develop into healthy adults. In some of our past physical education lessons we have learned and practiced sports skills such as dribbling a ball with the hands or rolling using stretched and curled motions. We have danced moving fast and slow and played games such as Zone Tag using chasing, fleeing, and dodging skills. These lessons have focused on learning to move more skillfully.

"Today our lesson is going to focus on being healthy and physically fit. We want to learn and think about how to help our bodies to be in good shape. When you hear the term *good shape*, what do you think people mean? What words would you use to describe a person who is in good shape? You have almost a minute to write down your ideas on your paper. [After approximately 1 minute] Who can tell me one of their ideas? I'm going to write these on the board [or chart paper] so everyone can see. Yes, Josh, *healthy* is a good word. Yes, Monika, strong body; look good, eat good foods. Yes, these are all good words for being in good shape! [Place checks by the responses that are repeated.]

"From your lists we have the idea that being in good shape has something to do with how the body is used and what the body can do. Also, being in shape is closely connected to how we feel. When you are in good shape, you have more energy, feel better, and don't tire out as easily.

"You also mentioned the idea of eating the right kinds of food and avoiding junk food. Later we'll learn more about healthy eating habits. For today let's think about physical activities that will help us to have a healthy body and to be in good shape.

[Write the words *active* and *inactive* on the board.] "What does *active* mean and how is it different from *inactive*? Yes, Tricia, you've got the idea. When we're doing something active the body is moving and working to do a task. We need more energy to do active tasks. When we are inactive the body doesn't move very much and we use less energy.

Now, let's list activities and tasks that are active and those that are inactive. You will work in your assigned groups, and each group will choose a recorder to write down your ideas on the paper. Your group has about 3 minutes to talk and list at least five activities for each term. [After several minutes have each recorder report the group's ideas. List the ideas on the board and check the ideas that are frequently mentioned. Probable responses for active tasks are playing, riding bikes, and playing sports and for inactive, watching TV, sleeping, and doing homework.]

"From our discussion, we have learned that if you are to be in good shape you must be active in your daily life. The key terms that we discussed today are *good shape, active,* and *inactive.* Let's think of active things that you can do during recess today. What are some active things? [Get responses and add ideas of your own like climbing on the playground equipment, playing tag, playing hopscotch, jumping rope.] See if you can do active things at recess today to help yourself to be in good shape! As you leave PE today, I want you to quickly tell me what you will do today to be active at recess. I'd like you to line up now and think of your activity!" [As students leave, have them quickly tell you their ideas.]

Look For

- When children are writing their lists of ideas walk around the room to look at responses and help children who are having difficulty.

- Check for understanding by calling on different individuals rather than letting children call out answers.

- During closure ask individual children to explain the key words of *good shape, active,* and *inactive.*

How Can I Change This?

- Have small groups start the class by listing ideas for being in good shape. Arrange for the classroom teacher to provide time for active tasks after the lesson.

> **TEACHABLE MOMENT**
>
> Relate being in good shape to doing active things so children can see the link between regular activity and feeling healthy.

HEALTH-RELATED CIRCUIT

Objectives

As a result of participating in this learning experience, children will improve their ability to

- identify the components of health-related fitness
- match activities and exercises with the appropriate fitness component
- demonstrate the correct and safe technique for each exercise (5-6, #22)

Suggested Grade Range

Intermediate (3–6)

Organization

Prepare signs and circuit stations (see Figure 6.5). This lesson can be done in a variety of spaces—gym, outside, even in a classroom if the lesson is modified.

Equipment Needed

Physical Best or similar poster listing health-related fitness components—cardiorespiratory endurance, muscular strength and endurance, body composition, and flexibility (see Figure 6.6); 2 sets of 7 activity signs—1 to identify stations in the circuit and the other set for the teacher to display; 1 carpet square, bench, or desk chair for each student.

Description

"In a previous lesson we learned that there are two kinds of fitness: health-related and skill-related. Can someone tell us the difference? Yes, Jamal, we need health-related fitness for our everyday activities. Good, Charise, to avoid getting sick (health problems)

Bench stepping   Jogging in place   Crunches   Push-ups (modified and regular)   Sit-ups   Stretching   Elbow presses

Figure 6.5   Diagram of health-related stations.

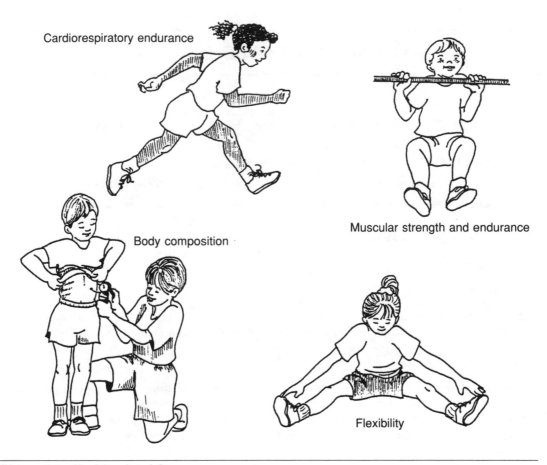

Cardiorespiratory endurance

Muscular strength and endurance

Body composition

Flexibility

Figure 6.6 Health-related fitness components.

because we aren't active. What about skill-related fitness? Yes, Matt, it means we have the fitness necessary to be skillful in sports, gymnastics, and dance.

"Today, we will learn more about the parts of health-related fitness and practice some activities we can use to improve each part, or what we call each "component." This poster [Figure 6.6] lists health-related fitness parts, or components, and gives a brief description of each one. Let's read the poster together. [Go over the components of cardiorespiratory endurance, muscular strength and endurance, body composition, and flexibility.] Now I'm going to cover the poster and I want you to check your understanding by turning to the person next to you to form partners. One of you start by trying to name the four health-related fitness components. Your partner can give you a clue if you can't remember. Then your partner gets to name them. Go. [After a couple of minutes] Everyone stop and look at me. Was any partner able to name all four of the components? Raise your hand if your partner could. Let's all say them together [uncover the poster again for all to see]. Hey, that's great! You can name all four of the health-related components.

"Now we will do some activities that help us improve each of the components. Look at the circuit stations as I explain them. [The students should have had previous instructions on correct technique for these exercises, with the possible exception of bench stepping. A quick review is helpful. Select a few students to demonstrate. In the case of new stations, like bench stepping, the teacher should demonstrate the correct technique and rhythm.]

"Either Mary and Steve or I will demonstrate each of the stations. I will start with Station 1, bench stepping. Watch as I keep a steady rhythm of up with the left foot, up with the right foot, down with the left foot and down with the right. The rhythm goes left, right, left, right. Second is push-ups. You can do the modified type with the knees down or the regular type with the knees up, but be sure to keep a straight back and bend your elbows, not your waist, to lower your body. Steve and Mary are doing them well. Sit-ups are the third station. Remember to bend your knees and fold your arms across your chest. If you can't lift all the way up then raise your shoulders off the floor, hold briefly, and ease back down. The fourth station is called elbow presses. It's a tough one! Support your weight on your hands and feet with your abdomen pointing up and hips lifted. Then point your fingers toward your feet and bend at the elbows to lower your body. Remember that your fingers face your feet and that you bend at the elbows only. Station 5 has several pictures of stretches [provide, for example, pictures of the hamstring sit-and-reach or lower-back stretches] for you to practice. Remember to gently stretch until you feel your muscles pull and hold the stretch for at least 15 slow counts. Jogging in place is at the sixth station. The key points for this activity are to lift your knees and keep a steady pace. The final station is called crunches. Watch them do this one. You lie on your back with feet crossed and legs lifted off the floor. Your knees should be bent and lined up over your hips. Then lift your head up toward your knees with your fingers supporting the sides of your head. There is a low bench here if you need it to support your feet while you lift your shoulders off the floor and tighten your abdominals. Notice how Mary and Steve are very controlled as they do this—no collapsing! Now you get a chance to try these. Once I send you to a station, do the exercise until you hear the signal to stop. Then go to the next highest station number. Those at the last station go back to Station 1. [Distribute students and allow about 30 to 40 seconds at each station; if time permits continue rotating through the circuit again.]

"Now that you've tried some fitness exercises, let's see if you can identify the fitness component that best matches the exercise. The fitness components on the poster are numbered from 1 to 4. When I say the name of an exercise, hold up the number of fingers to indicate the component that you think best matches it. That's right, number 2, muscular strength and endurance, matches with sit-ups. Why? Yes, Molly, because the muscles have to work hard to do all those sit-ups. And what muscles are helped by doing sit-ups? Yes, the abdominal muscles! What about jogging? Yes, Julia, it's for cardiorespiratory endurance. Why do you say that? Yes, your heart is beating faster and you start to sweat a little. What other station also improves cardiorespiratory endurance? Yes, Billy, bench stepping. What about push-ups? Good, that's for muscular strength and endurance—you really have to use your arm muscles! Elbow presses? Yes, Marcus, the same—muscular strength and endurance. And what about crunches? Good, Jeremy, muscular strength and endurance, too. What muscles work when you do this? Yes, your abdominals.

"Now, have you noticed that your responses have covered flexibility, cardiorespiratory endurance, and muscular strength and endurance, but that we haven't matched an exercise with body composition? We've learned already that body composition is the relationship of lean tissue like muscle to the amount of fat tissue in our body. If a person wanted to reduce the fat in the body, how could this be accomplished? Good, you remembered—through diet and exercise. Eat a balanced diet that is low in fatty foods. And do exercises that use the large muscles and move the whole body. Now, let's look at the exercises you did today. Which ones moved the whole body? Yes, bench stepping and jogging in place. Therefore, these exercises are not only good for cardiorespiratory or *aerobic* endurance, but also for improving your body composition. Think about trying some of these as you go home today. See you in 2 days!"

Look For

- Observe students to see if they perform exercises properly. If several students are performing incorrectly, stop the class and review with a demonstration. Give positive feedback or corrective feedback to individuals as needed.
- Can students identify the components of health-related fitness?
- Do students correctly match the components and exercises?

How Can I Change This?

- Use different exercises for the components such as jumping rope for cardiorespiratory endurance or bar push-ups for muscular strength and endurance. In subsequent lessons, repeat the circuit and give students more practice matching activities with components.

- Change the organizational format to provide a circle of activities so each student participates in a different fitness activity. Prepare laminated exercise cards and arrange them in a large circle with room for everyone in the class to have their own exercise cards and to be able to move safely. Line drawings or pictures on 5 × 7 file cards work well. Possible exercises include jumping jacks, lunges, squat thrusts, jogging in place, jumping rope, stretching exercises, push-ups, sit-ups, box jumping, hoop jumping, and the like. See Figure 6.7 for examples.

- Distribute students around the circle so they face inward. After about a minute have children rotate clockwise to the next activity card and continue several times or many times, depending on your purpose. You can use the Fitness Activity Circle as an instant activity or you can use it to reinforce the fitness components by matching the different fitness activities with the correct component. You can also challenge students to participate in this activity for a continuous period of time, such as 15 minutes.

- Modifications for the classroom: Select learning tasks that can be done in self-space, for example, jogging in place, sit-ups, push-ups. Do the selected tasks as a whole group rather than in stations. For example, demonstrate bench stepping on a chair, then have students use their own chairs for the stepping exercise. Proceed with sit-ups, push-ups, stretching activities, and other group tasks performed together to complete the Health-Related Circuit.

TEACHABLE MOMENT

Help children understand that many activities are helpful for more than one component. For example, bench stepping helps develop both the components of cardiorespiratory fitness and muscular endurance of the legs.

Figure 6.7 Fitness activity circle.

MAKING STRONGER MUSCLES

Objective

As a result of participating in this learning experience, children will improve their ability to

- describe the meaning of the terms *overload*, *repetitions*, and *sets* (5-6, #21)

Suggested Grade Range

Intermediate (3–6)

Organization

This lesson can be done in a variety of spaces—outside, inside, or in a classroom—with students scattered or at desks.

Equipment Needed

Chalkboard, chalk, and eraser or newsprint and markers

Description

"Remember how we described people who are in good shape in our last fitness lesson? You told me that they have healthy hearts and strong muscles, exercise regularly, and do activities that are fun and healthy. Can you tell me some of those healthy activities? Yes, basketball, soccer, jump rope, bike riding. What specific exercises will also help make your muscles stronger? Yes, sit-ups, push-ups, and crunches. The key words for today's lesson are *overload, repetitions* (also called *reps*), and *sets*. [List those words on the board or newsprint to refer to now and during the lesson.] During the lesson we will be doing overload, reps, and sets, so by the end you will know what these three words mean!

"In kindergarten and first grade you learned how to do exercises such as push-ups and sit-ups. Today we will learn to do them to make our muscles even stronger. Even in the classroom we can be active and enjoy moving. Remember to watch your space carefully. We will start today's class with some warm-up exercises that we've done before. Everyone find a personal space and begin walking in place. That's the way to spread out. Now continue with our warm-up. I'll do it too [or designate student leaders].

Walk in place. Stay with the beat, swing your arms, and lift your knees. Let's do this for 16 steps [16 counts].

Washing machine. Hands on hips, rotate back and forth saying swish swash one, swish swash two, and so on. Let's go for eight steps [8 counts].

Sky stretch. Reach in the air with one hand and arm and then the other eight times [8 counts].

Back stretch. Bend your knees, spread your feet, touch the floor with both hands, and straighten up to a standing position. Let's repeat this eight times. Go! [8 counts].

Walk in place one more time for 16 steps [16 counts].

High knee jog in place [32 counts].

Clap side to side [8 counts].

Imaginary rope jumping [8 counts].

Imaginary swim. Let's use the overhand crawl stroke 16 times [16 counts].

"Well done! Now that we've prepared our muscles for action, let's learn how to make our muscles stronger. First let's work on our arm and shoulder muscles by doing push-ups. You have a choice of doing 5, 8, or 10 push-ups—either full push-ups with your knees off the ground or modified push-ups with your knees on the ground. Decide which type and how many to do. Stand beside the person next to you and decide who will do the activity first. Now, one partner do their push-ups, full or knee, while the other partner counts. You can see that I am writing what we did on the board. [Write 5 repetitions on the board or chart paper.] Now the other partner should do their push-ups. Now everyone has done at least 5 *repetitions* of push-ups. We call this one *set* of 5; everyone has now done one set of push-ups. You should see that I have written '5 repetitions = 1 set' on the board because that is what we have just done. Instead of stopping we will overload the muscles and do 5 more push-ups, or one more set. The first partner go ahead and do 5 more push-ups and when you finish have the second partner do another set.

[After they are done] "You can decide how many repetitions and how many sets. Today we did two sets of 5 repetitions, but you can also do two sets of 10 repetitions or other combinations to suit your needs.

"What did we do after the first set of push-ups? That's right, we rested. But did we rest for long? No, right away we did another set of push-ups. That was called *overload*. The key word for overload is *more*. [Write the word *more* next to *overload* on the board.]

"The real key to increasing strength is that you warm up the muscles and work them until they are tired—and then do a little more. You may not be able to do 30 sit-ups at one time, but you probably can do 15, and rest briefly, and do 15 more.

"Now let's make our abdominal muscles stronger by doing sit-ups. [Have half the class do sit-ups while partners hold their feet and count and then switch roles.] How many repetitions did we do? Right, we did 15. How many sets of sit-ups have we done? Yes, 15 repetitions make one set. OK, now let's overload our muscles by doing another set of 15 sit-ups. [Repeat the sit-ups with both groups.]

"Let's review what we have learned today. [Cover up the board or newsprint.] One partner tell the other what *overload* means. Mario, what did your partner tell you? Yes, it means doing *more* than you usually do; working our muscles harder than normal. Now the other partner describe what we did today to make our muscles work harder. Natalie, tell the group. Right, we did repetitions and sets of push-ups and sit-ups."

Look For

- Look for correct performance of the activities so students use appropriate muscles. For example, push-ups should be done by bending the elbows with a straight back, buttocks up.

- Listen to responses when partners try to explain overload and reps and sets and take time to clarify these points.

How Can I Change This?

- Focus the lesson on overload and teach repetitions and sets in subsequent lessons. Adjust the number of repetitions to meet your children's needs. Try three sets instead of two. Use different activities such as biceps curls with an elastic hose.

Chapter 7

Learning Experiences for Cardiorespiratory Endurance

Cardiorespiratory endurance, frequently referred to as aerobic exercise, is an essential fitness component that must be introduced in enjoyable ways to children. Children are fascinated by learning about the heart, circulatory system, and respiratory system. Fortunately, there are numerous educational materials available to help you teach these important concepts (see Additional Resources). In this chapter you will find learning experiences that will help you teach some of the concepts associated with cardiorespiratory endurance. The following learning experiences are designed to teach children about the heart and circulatory system and how to achieve and maintain a healthy cardiorespiratory system.

Focus	Name	Suggested grade range
Location, size, and action of the heart	Listening to Your Heart	Pre-K–2
Meaning of and how to test cardiorespiratory endurance	Endurance Challenge	Pre-K–2
Atherosclerosis and the arteries	Keeping the Pipes Clean	3–6
Meaning and examples of aerobic activities	Run to the Front	3–6
Parts of the cardiorespiratory system and blood flow	Heart Pump Circuit	3–6
Participation in aerobic exercise	Fitness Club	1–6

LISTENING TO YOUR HEART

Objectives

As a result of participating in this learning experience, children will improve their ability to

- identify the location, size, and action of the heart
- listen to and identify the lub-dub sounds of the heart muscle at work (1-2, #25)
- listen to the response of the heart after rest and exercise (1-2, #25)

Suggested Grade Range

Primary (Pre-K–2)

Organization

Can be conducted in limited space, even a classroom. Establish partners. If possible before class starts, have a helper pass out one paper towel to each set of partners. Place one alcohol-soaked cotton swab on the towel.

Equipment Needed

1 stethoscope for every 2 children (sources: Purchase through a medical supply company. Some possibilities are Connecticut Valley Biological Supply Company, P.O. Box 326, 82 Valley Rd., Southampton, MA 01073 (1-800-628-7748); or Frey Scientific, 905 Hickory Ln., P.O. Box 8101, Mansfield, OH 44901-8101. Or you can borrow them from a local nursing school—university, community college, technical school. Check well in advance to schedule a time when stethoscopes are not in use); alcohol, cotton, and paper towels for cleaning stethoscopes; audiotape of heart sounds (source: American Heart Association Schoolsite Program's lower elementary education kit); tape recorder.

Description

"Imagine all the wonderful things that go on inside your body. One of the most amazing facts is that our hearts are always working to pump blood to our muscles so we can play and exercise.

"Hold up your fist. This is the size of your heart. Put your fist over where you think your heart is. That's right, it is slightly to the left side of your chest.

"The heart is a very strong muscle, and it is always beating while you are alive. Without a heart, we wouldn't be alive! That's why it is important to know what the heart does and how to take care of it.

"I am going to play a recording of the sound of the heart, so listen carefully. You will hear two sounds. See if you can tell how they are different. [Play the heartbeat recording.] Raise your hand if you could hear the two different sounds. One is softer and the other is stronger. The first sound, the soft sound, is called *lub*. The second sound, stronger, is called *dub*. The *lub-dub* sounds are made by the blood going in and being pumped out of the heart. Say the two sounds with me—lub-dub, lub-dub, lub-dub.

"Now we will all get a chance to use a stethoscope, just like a doctor or nurse uses to listen to our heart. I will show you how to use the stethoscope and those of you who are quiet and listening will get to try it. First, use the alcohol swab to clean the stethoscope's earplugs before each partner uses it. Clean it each time. Then carefully place the stethoscope over your partner's heart and listen to the sounds. Begin as soon as I give you the stethoscope. [Distribute the stethoscopes and assist children.]

"You've been listening to the heart while sitting down. Now let's do some exercise and listen to what happens. When I give the start signal, one of the partners get up and jog in place. I'll time you for 1 minute. [After 1 minute] Now stop and stand still so the other partner can use the stethoscope to listen to your heart. What happened? Why is the heart beating faster? Yes, you were moving and exercising! [More advanced answers include that the muscles need more energy so the heart has to pump more blood to them. The blood carries oxygen to the muscles.] Now have the other partner try exercising. [You can choose any appropriate exercise, such as sit-ups or jumping rope.] Then sit down and let your partner listen to your heart.

[When done] "While Sherry and Alicia carefully collect the stethoscopes and materials, I'm going to ask you a few questions. Quietly raise your hand if you think you know the answer. [Pause after each question so everyone has a chance to think about the answer.] First, what is the heart? Yes, Adam, it is a muscle. What does the heart do? Good, it pumps blood. Why does your body need a heart? This is harder. It needs one to pump blood to your muscles and body to keep it alive. What happens to the heart when you exercise? Yes, Crystal, it beats faster. Everyone show me how big your heart is. That's right, about the size of your fist. And where is it located? Show me with your hand. [Check that children place hands on the left center of the chest.] And last, everyone make the sound of the heart. I'm hearing lub-dub, lub-dub, lub-dub. Good! Stop. Well done! We'll do some healthy heart exercises in our next lesson. Look forward to it—it'll be fun. See you later."

Look For

- After handing out the stethoscopes, observe closely to see that children are using them safely and properly. If not, stop the class immediately and address the problems you observed.
- Do children form a fist and place it over the left side of the chest?
- Do they correctly identify the heart as a muscle?
- Do they notice the increase in heart rate after exercise?
- Can they explain why the heart pumps faster during exercise?

How Can I Change This?

- Open and close the fist repeatedly to simulate the continuous and difficult pumping action of the heart. Use two hands to simulate the heart opening and closing to receive blood and pump it out.
- Count the number of heartbeats during rest and after exercise for a specific time like 20 seconds. Compare and discuss why they are different.

TEACHABLE MOMENT

Feel the heartbeat pulse on the wrist and on the carotid artery in the neck. Discuss the fact that the heart is pumping blood forcefully through the arteries so we can feel the pulse on various parts of the body. When children state that the heart pumps blood, ask why. You can discuss basic facts such as the need for nutrients and oxygen and the process of removing waste products.

ENDURANCE CHALLENGE

Objectives

As a result of participating in this learning experience, children will improve their ability to

- test their cardiorespiratory endurance
- explain the meaning of cardiorespiratory endurance

Suggested Grade Range

Primary (Pre-K–2)

Organization

Running track or large marked area, 200 yards for one lap

Equipment Needed

12 marking cones, watch, 6 plastic straws for each student

Description

"Today we'll see if you're like the Energizer bunny—if you can keep going and going and going. First, does anyone know what the word *endurance* means? What is a person with a lot of endurance able to do? Well, it means you are able to use your muscles for a long time without getting very tired.

"The purpose of today's lesson is to find out the endurance of your heart, lungs, and muscles by seeing how far you can go in 10 minutes. We'll be doing this by counting how many times you can go around the track marked off by the cones. You'll start here, at this line [show] and keep moving by walking, running, even skipping for 10 minutes. After each lap I will give you a straw, so when the time is up you can see how many laps you've completed. Remember, start out slowly so you can keep moving for the full 10 minutes. If you start out too fast, you'll be too pooped to keep moving. Think of the Energizer bunny—he doesn't go too fast or too slow. After I blow the whistle to stop, I'll write down how many straws you collected.

"Right now I'd like the people who have birthdays in January, February, March, or April to come up and begin . . . now, May, June, July, and August . . . now, September, October, November, and December. [Give signal to go and begin timing. Encourage students during the 10 minutes and remind them to pace themselves. Hand out straws each time they pass the start line; at the end of 10 minutes, use the whistle to signal students to stop.]

"Everyone come on over here . . . I'm going to let you go on over to the playground while I write down the number of straws you have. Listen for your name, I will call it out; when I do, you need to come over to me quickly. Go. [Call students over one at a time to collect their straws and write down the number of straws each had. When done, call all students in to you.]

"Everyone stop what you are doing and safely come to our meeting circle. Listen to my question and raise your hand if you have an answer. What were we working on today? Yes, Sharise, our endurance. If you were able to do one, two, or three laps, you're off to a good start! If you could do four or five laps, you have good endurance. If you had six or more straws, you had super endurance! Does anyone remember what it means to have good endurance? Yes, Bobby, it means that we can keep going and going and going—that our muscles and heart and lungs could work for a long time without getting tired. What are some ways that you can work on your endurance at home? Yes, Shiloh, you can jog and run fast. What else? Yes, Barb, you can play tag and swim. Let's keep the other answers for next time—you can tell me what you did to help your endurance. Good job today working on your endurance!"

Look For

- Children who lack pacing. Discuss this with the whole class or just with the individuals who have trouble.
- Children who do a good job of maintaining an even pace throughout the challenge should be reinforced for their efforts.

How Can I Change This?

- Focus this learning experience on fitness walking. Use the "Straw Walk" activities from Creative Walking Incorporated (see Additional Resources).
- Challenge the children to keep moving by running or walking for the full time.
- Use a longer time for the challenge, for example, use 15 minutes in a future lesson.
- For intermediate children (grades 3 to 6), change the rules to stress continuous jogging for the full time. Have students predict how long they can keep jogging and challenge them to achieve their predictions. Establish a rule that if students have to stop jogging they must go to an alternate activity area for the remainder of the time. Jumping rope or climbing on playground equipment are possible alternatives.

TEACHABLE MOMENT

If some children start out very fast and then have to stop or walk, discuss the benefits of pacing. Discuss how students can improve their personal time for jogging by practicing walking and jogging every day. Improvement will come from walking and jogging during recess and with their friends and family at home.

KEEPING THE PIPES CLEAN

Objectives

As a result of participating in this learning experience, children will improve their ability to

- explain the effects of atherosclerosis on the arteries
- identify regular exercise and proper nutrition as ways to help prevent atherosclerosis (3-4, #24)

Suggested Grade Range

Intermediate (3–6)

Organization

To begin class, have students sitting down for instruction. Organize equipment and space for an aerobic activity.

Equipment Needed

1 rusty pipe with obvious obstructions, 1 clean pipe with a smooth inner surface, poster of the circulatory system from American Heart Association. Optional: Record player/music box, or aerobic exercise videotape for warm-up activity

Description

"Before starting our aerobic activity for the day we are going to see what happens to our blood vessels when we take care of our body and what happens when we don't take care of it. The poster shows the blood vessels in our body that carry oxygen and nutrients to our muscles. The large red vessels around the heart are called coronary arteries. They are very important because they supply blood to the heart muscle to keep us alive.

"I want to show you what happens to these arteries if we don't take care of them. [Show the rusty pipe.] This old, rusty pipe is like an artery that hasn't been taken care of. Our blood vessels are like pipes except that real vessels are soft and flexible, like a garden hose. What do you think happens to the pipe when it is not cleaned out? Yes, Fernando, your arteries can get clogged up like this old pipe, so the blood has a hard time getting through. We call this hardening of the arteries and it makes the heart work harder. Too much clogging can even stop the flow of blood and cause a heart attack and death. [Show the new, clean pipe.] Now, look at the clean pipe that has been taken care of. Which pipe would you like to have? What do you think we can do to take care of our own 'pipes?' [Allow for some responses.] That's right, Jenna, we can take care of our pipes by doing aerobic exercise. Yes, Harley, we can eat low-cholesterol and low-fat foods. Now let's have some fun and help our vessels at the same time by doing a neat aerobic activity. [Choose an aerobic exercise routine from Kimbo Educational or the Florida Fit to Achieve Video. See Additional Resources for references. We recommend 'Ghostbusters' from Jackie Sorenson's Aerobic Club for Kids from Kimbo Educational.]

[When done] "What type of exercise have we done today? That's right, aerobic exercise to music. It's fun and it keeps our pipes clean! *Atherosclerosis* is a big word used to describe clogging of the arteries like this old rusty pipe. Remember that continuous exercise makes our hearts beat faster and increases our breathing so it helps the arteries around our heart stay strong, open, and healthy. What we eat is also very important, so we'll discuss that on another day."

Look For

- Can students explain that atherosclerosis means hardening and clogging of the arteries? Do students prefer the clean pipe? Can they explain why exercise and diet help keep the vessels open?

How Can I Change This?

- Use water to represent the blood and pour it through the two pipes to show how the flow is easy in the "healthy" pipe and obstructed in the "unhealthy" pipe.

TEACHABLE MOMENT

The poster of the circulatory system will stimulate questions about the body. Ask why aerobic exercise would help keep the vessels in good shape. (It strengthens the heart muscle and forces more blood through the vessels.)

RUN TO THE FRONT

Objectives

As a result of participating in this learning experience, children will improve their ability to

- explain the meaning of aerobics
- identify activities that are considered aerobic exercise (5-6, #23)

Suggested Grade Range

Intermediate (3–6)

Organization

Use cones or markers to set off a 200-yard oval or rectangular route for children to travel around (Figure 7.1).

Equipment Needed

14 cones, whistle, poster (Figure 7.2) with illustrations to display terms and definitions

Description

"Look at this poster [Figure 7.2] while I review some information we will be learning today. We know that our muscles need oxygen to make energy so we can work and play. *Aerobics* means any activity that makes our muscles use oxygen for a continuous period of time. Aerobic activities and exercises improve the endurance of our heart and lungs. Our poster shows some aerobic activities, such as walking, roller skating, and swimming.

"Today, we are going to participate in an aerobic activity called Run to the Front that will help improve our cardiorespiratory endurance. We will do the activity in a group. [Set up groups of 4 to 6 children ahead of time so children of similar aerobic endurance and pacing speed are in the same group. Call out each group, then have one group come up to demonstrate while others sit and watch.] The group will begin by walking around the track or course in a single file formation, closely following each other around the markers. When you hear the signal [one whistle] the last person in line must run to the front of the line and then resume walking. You will use other ways to travel too, such as skipping, hopping, crab walking, walking backwards, sliding,

Figure 7.1   Diagram of running to the front.

Aerobics means *with oxygen*.

Oxygen is needed by the muscles to make energy
for work and play.

Aerobic endurance: when heart and lungs supply oxygen to
the muscles so the whole body can work for a continuous
period of time —15 minutes to an hour or more.

Aerobic activities:

Walking	Jogging	Roller Skating
Bicycling	Swimming	Dancing
Tag Games	Soccer	Basketball

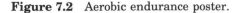

Figure 7.2   Aerobic endurance poster.

and jogging. I will call these out and you'll need to change your movement when I do.
[Start all the groups out slightly separated and walking around the course. Use the
signal for running to the front and give everyone an opportunity to lead. Then periodically call out a change in travel. After 10 to 15 minutes have all groups sit down and
stretch for closure.]

"What parts of your body were you using most during this activity? That's right, we
used the large muscles, legs, heart, and lungs. Run to the Front is an example of what
type of activity? Yes, Kendra, aerobic endurance. How can you tell if an activity is
aerobic? Good! An aerobic activity uses large muscles and whole-body actions to travel
and it increases our heartbeat and breathing for a long period of time."

Look For

- Do students stay in a single file formation and use the designated mode of travel?
  If not, have the group or individual take a time-out to observe the appropriate action.

- Are the students cooperating with each other to do the tasks appropriately? If not,
  have the group sit down to discuss this problem. You may want to have a cooperative
  group once again illustrate how the members work together. Are students physically
  able to maintain the activity? If not, use movements that are less vigorous.

- Can children identify the criteria for an aerobic activity?

How Can I Change This?

- Use traveling movements that are easier or harder, depending on your students'
  ability and interests. For example, use only walking or only jogging.

- If students' fitness levels are low and they need to develop stamina, begin with 5 to
  7 minutes of sustained activity and gradually increase to 15 minutes.

- Vary the area or terrain used for traveling. Eventually a teacher-directed signal is
  not necessary and groups can play Run to the Front at their own pace. Discuss pacing
  and explain that the idea is for each group to stay together as a pack, not leaving
  anyone behind or allowing anyone to go out ahead. Make sure each person in the
  group has a turn to lead the pack during a 10-minute pacing exercise. Give each
  group a different starting place around the rectangles and post signs to indicate

when to walk and jog. Each time the pack returns to its starting point, the present leader raises a hand to signal for the last person to jog to the front and become the new leader.

TEACHABLE MOMENTS

During the activity, have students pause to feel their pulse and monitor their breathing rates. Ask why they are increasing (more oxygen is necessary to keep going).

Why are some people breathing harder than others? (Discuss individual differences in the ability of the heart and lungs to deliver oxygen to the muscles.)

HEART PUMP CIRCUIT

Objectives

As a result of participating in this learning experience, children will improve their ability to

- identify the different parts of the cardiovascular system
- describe the flow of blood from the heart to the body (muscles), back to the heart and the lungs, and to the heart and the body again

Suggested Grade Range

Intermediate (3–6)

Organization

The heart pump circuit as shown in Figure 7.3 must be set up prior to class in a space large enough for your whole class of children to move around in. The circuit represents major components of the circulatory system by boxes, hoops, and rope tunnels. Oxygen and carbon dioxide are represented by tennis balls and racquetball balls.

Equipment Needed

2 cardboard boxes (lungs), 8 long ropes (vessels), 2 hoops (heart pumps), 1 bicycle tire pump (heart pumping action), 20 racquetball balls (carbon dioxide), 20 tennis balls (oxygen), poster of circulatory system from American Heart Association, 1 heart pump worksheet (see Figure 7.4) for each student

Description

"You know that the heart pumps blood but do you know where the blood goes when it leaves the heart? Today, you will actually travel the path of the blood through the body. We call this the circulatory system.

"First look at the picture of the circulatory system [use a poster from the American Heart Association and point out the main components]. We have a circuit set up on the floor today to symbolize these parts of the circulatory system. We'll call it the heart pump circuit because the heart has two pumps. One side pumps blood to the lungs and the other side pumps blood to the body.

"The red blood vessels are called arteries. They carry oxygen to the muscles so that energy can be produced. The blue vessels are called veins. They carry carbon dioxide to the lungs, and it leaves your body when you breathe out. The heart makes all this possible by pumping the blood through both types of blood vessels.

"We'll need some of you to help play the parts of the heart pump circuit. One person will use the tire pump and play the part of the heart. You will pretend to pump the blood just like the heart does. Then another person will play the part of the lungs by taking the carbon dioxide, these racquetballs, and giving oxygen, the tennis balls. Another person will stand at the body parts poster and take oxygen and give carbon dioxide as the blood passes through.

"Now watch as Jeremy and Joanne go through the circuit. You'll start at the heart pump and get pumped to the lungs. There you will give up carbon dioxide—a racquet-ball—and pick up oxygen—a tennis ball. Then you'll come back to the left side of the heart and be pumped through the vessels to the area for the body parts and cells. Here you will give up oxygen and pick up carbon dioxide and carry it through the vessels back to the right side of the heart. From here the circuit repeats itself. You will start

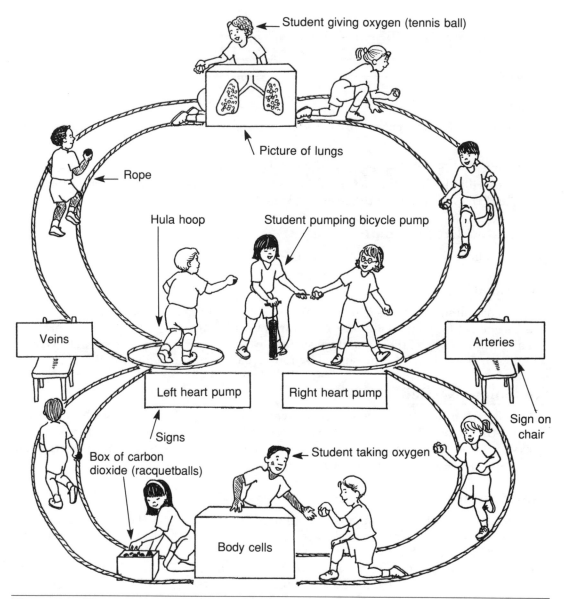

Figure 7.3 Heart pump circuit.

at the lung pump and keep moving through the circuit until I tell you to stop. As you travel through the heart pump circuit I'll ask you to identify where you are in the circulatory system. At times I'll stop the whole class and check your knowledge by asking questions like 'Raise your hand if you are in the arteries,' or 'Jump up and down if you are blood carrying oxygen!' Ready?" [Start a few children at a time and monitor their progress; gradually introduce students to the circuit until all students are participating. After they've gone through the circuit several times, have them go to another area to start filling out the heart pump worksheet (Figure 7.4) to reinforce the lesson objectives.]

Look For

• Can children identify the part of the circulatory system they are traveling through? Can they correctly fill out the heart pump worksheet?

How Can I Change This?

• Focus only on the path of the blood by eliminating the oxygen and carbon dioxide and simplifying the worksheet.

Heart Pump and Blood Flow Worksheet

Label the parts of the heart pump circuit. Write the correct answer in the blank. Use the *Key Words* to help with spelling.

Key Words

capillaries   lungs   body   veins   arteries

2. _____

1. The heart pumps blood to the
_____.

3. The heart pumps blood to the
_____.

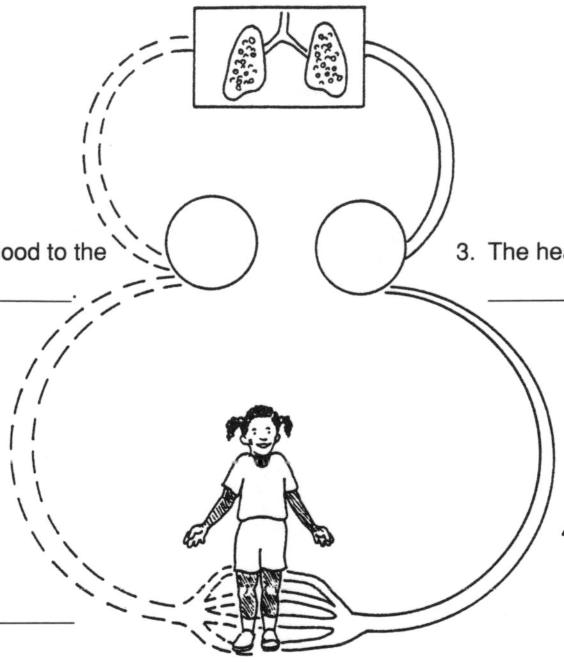

4. _____

6. _____

5. _____
give oxygen to the body parts and cells.

= = = = =

Blood without oxygen

——————

Blood with oxygen   Name _____

Figure 7.4   Heart pump and blood flow worksheet.

- Have the classroom teacher follow up by helping children complete the worksheet. Use the worksheet as a homework assignment.
- In a subsequent lesson change this experience to focus on the role of oxygen instead of on blood flow and call this the Oxygen Circuit. Add a hoop to travel through to represent the mouth and have children carry oxygen from the lungs to the heart and then to the muscles. You can use one, two, or three tennis balls to symbolize different amounts of oxygen. At the muscles have children exchange oxygen for an equivalent

amount of exercise, printed on a card. After doing the exercises the students pick up carbon dioxide (racquetball balls) and carry it back to the heart and then to the lungs to be removed from the body. Students will learn that as more oxygen is transported to the muscles, more energy is available to perform activities.

TEACHABLE MOMENT

Ask questions to develop understanding of the circulatory system. For example, "Why does the blood flow to the lungs?" (to get rid of carbon dioxide and pick up fresh oxygen), and "What does the blood carry?" (oxygen and nutrients for the cells, carbon dioxide and waste products). During other physical education activities ask children to think about the heart pump circuit and ask questions to link exercise and the heart actions.

FITNESS CLUB

Objectives

As a result of participating in this learning experience, children will improve their ability to

- sustain continuous running and walking (3-4, #14)
- identify walking and running as beneficial cardiorespiratory activities (5-6, #23)
- participate in daily walking and running outside of regularly scheduled physical education class time (5-6, #28)
- achieve fitness goals

Suggested Grade Range

Primary and Intermediate (1–6)

Organization

Meet with the school principal to explain the purpose of the Fitness Club and discuss procedures. Afterward meet with the classroom teachers to explain the purpose and procedures and request their help with the recording charts. Decide on procedures for recording laps before you start the club. Design a running and walking trail on the school grounds convenient to the school that is safe, accessible, and easily monitored. The size and type of your fitness trail will be influenced by the space available. Mark the trail with permanent fixtures, such as tires or posts in the ground or arrows painted on the cement. A half mile is an ideal distance, but trail distance can vary depending on the available land. If possible it should travel through some trees and varied terrain. Make some posters to use for introducing the club to students that explain the purpose, rules, and goals of the club and show examples of motivational certificates (see Figure 7.5). Take one class period to introduce the Fitness Club to children. Explain the purpose and the rules and display the goals and certificates. After explaining the details of the Fitness Club, finish the class by having everyone go around the trail at least once. This gives all students a chance to get started in the club. Thereafter, give students occasional opportunities to use the fitness trail during class time, but the purpose of

Seminole Fitness Club
10 Miles

Seminole Elementary School

Congratulations on achieving your goal!

Regular running and walking does many good things for your body. You are improving your physical fitness by strengthening your heart, lungs, blood vessels, and muscles and maintaining a normal body weight. Daily exercise is a terrific way to relax and relieve some of your tension. You can enjoy the company of others while running. You are on your way to a lifetime of health and fitness.

Figure 7.5   Sample Fitness Club certificate.

this club is to encourage activity outside of class time and should not take up time needed to meet other curriculum goals. If you start the club in the fall, it can continue throughout the school year.

Equipment Needed

Tires or posts to mark the fitness trail; award certificates (see Figure 7.5 for an example) printed on card stock (plan for 1 certificate for every student for the initial two awards, 5 and 10 mile, and don't put a date on them so you can use the leftover certificates the next year); poster showing the possible mileage goals and awards; memo to teachers, staff, and parents (see Figure 7.6 for an example).

Description

"This is the first day of our school Fitness Club. The purpose is to encourage you to participate in regular walking and jogging outside of our regularly scheduled physical education class time. Today after I explain the rules you'll all go at least once around the Fitness Club trail. This is a voluntary activity. You don't have to join. We want you to choose to exercise for fun and health benefits, not because someone else tells you to do it. What do you think are some benefits you can get from walking or running? Yes, Brent, your heart gets stronger. Good, Brynne, your endurance increases. Yes, Brooke, we can also make friends when we walk with others.

"Now, the rules are that you can run and walk the course at any time, but another person must see you go around the trail. Your teacher will have the Fitness Club chart in the classroom and will tell you when the laps will be recorded [it helps to have a responsible person record laps only at designated times during the day]. Once around our fitness trail is one quarter of a mile. You can only count four laps a day [start with

---

Memo: To Parents, Teachers, and Staff

From: The Elementary Physical Education Teachers

Regarding: Seminole Fitness Club

Purpose: We are starting a fitness club at this school to encourage participation in regular aerobic exercise. Aerobic exercise involves using oxygen to make energy and elevating the heart rate for a sustained period of time, which increases the fitness of the lungs, heart, and circulatory system. We will use walking and jogging as our means of exercise, since they require little equipment and can be enjoyed throughout one's lifetime.

Participation: All students in grades kindergarten through sixth and interested adults at this school. The program is voluntary and designed to reward all participants regardless of ability level.

Organization: The fitness club will continue for the remainder of the year. Participants may walk or jog the course at recess, physical education, or any time that the teacher determines. Students will record the number of laps they complete daily on a fitness club chart in their classrooms. When a certificate goal is reached, the student will receive the appropriate certificate.

When beginning to exercise, a gradual increase in the amount of work is best. Therefore, the kindergarten and first graders may do up to two laps a day. The second through fifth graders may do up to four laps a day. _____ laps equal one mile. The number of laps may be increased later after students build up adequate endurance.

Awards: 10 Mile Club, 25 Mile Club, 50 Mile Club, 100 Mile Club

How you can help: Participate yourself!

Discuss the benefits of regular exercise: cardiorespiratory fitness (a strong heart and lungs), weight control, walking and jogging with friends, accomplishing a goal, and enjoyment of exercise.

Figure 7.6 Sample Fitness Club memo to parents, teachers, and staff.

1 mile and later move up to 2 miles] because the best way to exercise is to do some each day, but not too much. You must have another person see you go around the trail for several reasons. One is that we want to encourage you to talk and be with friends when you exercise. It's fun to exercise with other people. It's also a good safety procedure to have someone else around when you exercise. And it will help everyone be honest about the number of laps you mark on the chart. When you reach one of the goals (5, 10, 25, 50 miles) then your teacher will give me your name and you will be awarded a certificate for a job well done! It will look like this [show sample as in Figure 7.5]. I'll give these out once a week on Fridays. Now that you know about the club, I want everyone to go with me around the trail and stay together this first time [have the whole class walk and jog around the Fitness Club trail so you can point out the exact route and no one is left behind].

"Today everyone will get credit for one lap. Now it's up to you to take some of your recess and free time to run and walk the trail. Find a friend and enjoy it!"

Look For

- Do children voluntarily participate in the club? If not, spend some time in class emphasizing the benefits and encouraging them. Reinforce those children who are participating.

- Are some children cheating on their laps? If so have a one-on-one talk to let them know you are aware of it and stress the meaning of achieving goals fairly and honestly. If this is unsuccessful, you can put the child on probation for a period of time.

- Do the classroom teachers have a workable system to record laps? This is very important because if the club is a hassle for the teachers then they won't encourage students to participate and they may even discourage them. Find out from teachers how it is working and share the good ideas they've thought of with other teachers. An occasional memo to update progress and communicate tips will be well received.

How Can I Change This?

- You can announce award winners on the school intercom and have them come to the office for their certificates. You can start the club as part of your physical education program and later expand to involvement with the classroom teachers. Add other activity stations around the Fitness Club trail such as muscular strength and endurance and flexibility exercises.

TEACHABLE MOMENT

Before or after participating in the Fitness Club, review terms such as *aerobics, cardiorespiratory endurance, FIT principles*, and *pacing*. Take opportunities to discuss the following benefits of participating in the Fitness Club: improving cardiorespiratory endurance, healthy heart exercise, socializing with friends, relieving stress, using calories to maintain body weight, accomplishing goals.

Chapter 8

Learning Experiences for Muscular Strength and Endurance

Many muscular strength and endurance activities and learning experiences can be integrated with other units of instruction. For example, dance and gymnastics lessons offer opportunities to have children practice taking weight on their hands in step-like actions (Purcell, 1994; Werner, 1994). Muscular strength and endurance exercises can be practiced for short periods of time as part of lessons on skills that depend on muscular strength. If you use exercises in this manner it is important to point out to children the link between this fitness component and successful performance.

Muscular strength and endurance exercises offer excellent opportunities for instant activities at the beginning of class (Graham, 1992). For example, you could have carpet squares out and students could go to them immediately and start partner sit-ups or you could have children work on their arm and shoulder strength by practicing climbing, hanging, and swinging on the playground apparatus.

This chapter presents sample learning experiences to help children learn information about and participate in activities that promote the health-related fitness components of muscular strength and endurance.

Focus	Name	Suggested grade range
How muscles get stronger; relating exercises to specific muscles	Muscle Time	Pre-K–2
Meaning of muscular strength and endurance	The Muscle Circuit	3–6
Identifying major muscle groups	Muscle of the Month	3–6

MUSCLE TIME

Objectives

As a result of participating in this learning experience, children will improve their ability to

- explain that muscles get stronger with regular use (1-2, #25)
- perform a variety of muscular strength and endurance activities correctly

Suggested Grade Range

Primary (Pre-K–2)

Organization

Set up muscular strength and endurance stations to include some upper body, abdominal, and leg activities. See Figures 8.1, 8.2, and 8.3 for activity ideas. Have enough stations so all children can participate without any waiting.

Equipment Needed

The activities you choose will determine the type of equipment you need. Use permanent playground apparatus if possible. We suggest horizontal bars, climbing platforms, milk jug weights, ropes to jump over, and mats for sit-ups and curl-ups. Also, signs for stations and a tambourine are needed.

Description

"Show me a muscle in your arm. That's right! Where else do you have a muscle? Yes, Gina, in our legs. That's right, Chris, in our necks. We have hundreds of muscles all over our body. How do you think we can make our muscles stronger? Right, by doing exercises and using our muscles everyday! We have many activities for you to practice today.

Figure 8.1   Examples of upper body muscular strength and endurance activities.

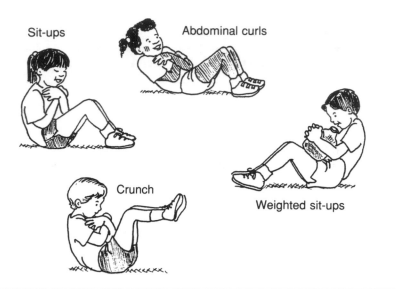

Figure 8.2 Examples of abdominal strength and endurance activities.

Figure 8.3 Examples of leg strength and endurance activities.

"Melissa and Grant are going to help me explain the six stations to you. Each station is marked with a numbered sign. Melissa, show how to do station 1 by climbing across the horizontal bars. When you get across, jog around to the beginning and do it again. Station 2 is sit-ups. Do as many as you can with your knees bent and your arms folded across your shoulders, just like Grant is doing now. At station 3 you will jump in and out of the hoops, then jog back to the start and do it again. Station 4 is push-ups. You can do them with your knees down, like Melissa is demonstrating, or with your knees off the ground. Well done, Melissa! At station 5 you will climb around and through the climbing platform. Finally, at station 6 you will practice using your leg muscles by jumping over the river formed by the two ropes. You can choose the distance you want to jump.

"When I call your name go to the station I indicate and start right away. When you hear the tambourine, stop, put the equipment away if necessary, and wait for my signal to move to the next station. [Distribute children to all the stations and then observe and

encourage continuous activity. After about 2 minutes, have children change stations.]
"Today you've exercised your muscles. How can we make our muscles stronger? Right, we have to use them every day! Next class we'll continue Muscle Time so you can practice all the activities."

Look For

- Observe and help children learn to perform the activities correctly. Be ready to modify these activities for children who cannot be successful otherwise.

How Can I Change This?

- Change the activities for variety. Use the Fitness Activity Circle (see Figure 6.7). List muscular strength and endurance activities on 5 × 8 inch file cards and laminate them. Have one card for every student by repeating some exercises if necessary. Before class put the cards out in a large circle with any necessary equipment. Children start at one card and rotate to another every minute on a signal.

- Introduce a Monkey Bar Club during a class period and encourage students to practice during recess and at other times during the day. Giving children some time during physical education classes to practice their climbing helps get the club going. This is an excellent instant activity (Graham, 1992) to use to start a class, and it can also be used to end a class. Just be sure to reinforce the message that regular climbing will strengthen the arm and shoulder muscles. You will need horizontal ladders for this activity—the more the better. To become a member of the club students must make one complete trip across the horizontal ladder. You can have a one-trip club or encourage continued practice by recognizing two or more trips. If a complete trip is unrealistic for some children then you can negotiate a goal of achieving so many rungs to be a member of the club. During selected physical education classes anyone interested in joining the club can demonstrate while you are watching. Figure 8.4 shows how you can display the names of club members on charts in the cafeteria or hallway.

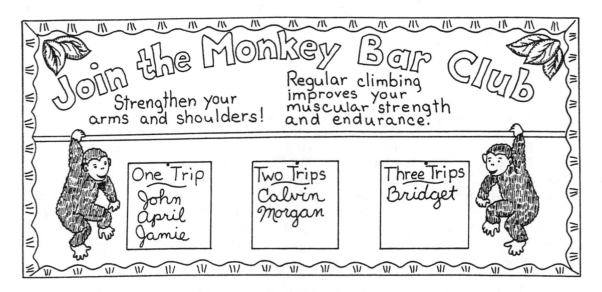

Figure 8.4 Monkey Bar Club poster.

TEACHABLE MOMENT

While children are involved at their stations you can ask individual children questions about which muscles they are using and making stronger.

THE MUSCLE CIRCUIT

Objectives

As a result of participating in this learning experience, children will improve their ability to

- identify the meaning of muscular strength and muscular endurance (5-6, #21)
- participate in and give examples for activities that improve muscular strength and endurance
- match activities with specific muscle groups—upper body, abdominal, and legs

Suggested Grade Range

Intermediate (3–6)

Organization

Use standard playground equipment and add other stations with signs to indicate desired activities such as sit-ups, horizontal ladder climb, bar push-ups, modified pull-ups, standing long jump, and jump the stick. See Figures 8.1, 8.2, and 8.3 for ideas.

Equipment Needed

Visual aids (a poster with pictures cut from magazines to define and illustrate muscular strength and endurance activities), signs for stations (use marking cones or sign boards to post the names of activities; numbers on the signs make the transition easier for younger children), whistle, soft landing areas with distance markings for long jump, 10 carpet squares for sit-ups and modified push-ups, 5 dowel sticks or tubes with 4 × 4 blocks to elevate them off the ground, and rope or markings for standing long jump

Description

"Today, we will be learning more about a component of fitness called muscular strength and endurance. Muscular strength means the amount of force your muscles can exert or give in a short period of time using maximum, or your biggest, effort [refer to a picture of lifting a weight or doing a pull-up], and endurance means the ability of your muscles to keep on working for long periods of time, repeating an effort many times. [refer to a picture of bicycling]. Muscular endurance is like being the Energizer Bunny—your muscles keep going and going and going. We will be practicing activities today that help both muscular strength and endurance. We will also be learning that different activities improve strength and endurance of specific parts of the body—the legs, abdominals, and upper body.

"While you are all sitting down, turn your palms up and circle your arms backward. What muscles are we exercising? Tony says the arms. Someone else said the shoulders. That's right, we are using the arm and shoulder muscles. Now let's stand up and do bicep curls. Start with your arms hanging down, palms facing out. Now bring your hands up to your shoulders and then back to the starting position [see Figure 8.1]. Good. And now the pect presses. Start with both arms held up and elbows bent. Now press both hands and forearms together, then move them apart, and repeat [see Figure 8.1]. All these are exercises for the upper body muscles. Watch me do an exercise for the leg muscles [demonstrate]. This is called a lunge. Now you try it. Start by standing with both feet together. Extend your right foot out like you are taking a long step. Now bend your left knee until it nearly touches the floor. Come back to the starting position and repeat, this time extending your left foot first and bending your right knee [see

Figure 8.3]. That's good. Now try lunging to the other side with the other leg. We've done exercises for the upper body muscles and the legs; now curl up on your back and do several crunches.

"Look at the signs set up around the playground. Each sign is for a different activity and you will be able to try these today. Now watch as Jenny demonstrates the activities that are new today. At station 1 Jenny is showing how to do the standing long jump. Remember to start with both feet together, bend your knees, swing your arms back, and explode into the air. Station 2 is the sit-up area, where you can do several variations of sit-ups—curl-ups, regular sit-ups, or sit-ups with a weight. What muscles are the sit-ups for? That's right, abdominals! We are going to do modified push-ups and push-ups with the knees off the ground at station 3. At station 4, Jenny is going to place the plastic tube on the two blocks and then try to jump back and forth over the tube. Station 5 is called bar push-ups. Jenny, show the class how to do them correctly, keeping the back straight. And station 6 is the horizontal ladder climb. Are there any questions? Remember, when I blow the whistle, sit down next to your station and listen for the signal to go to the next station. OK, you four go to station 1 and start. [Distribute children into equal groups and have each group begin their activity. After about 2 minutes give your stop signal (whistle) and have the groups rotate to the next station.]

[When done] "What was the purpose of today's activities? Yes, all the activities helped build muscular strength and endurance. What does muscular strength mean? Paul has the answer—it's our maximum muscular effort for a short period of time. What does muscular endurance mean? Good! You remembered that endurance means being able to use our muscles for a long time.

"Let's look at some examples of activities that require healthy levels of muscular strength and endurance. [Show poster with cut-out pictures from magazines. Good examples of activities to include are the iron cross on rings, chin-up, rock or wall climbing, bicycle racing, long jump, and Olympic weight lifting.]

"Although some activities require you to have lots of muscular strength *and* endurance, I want you to decide whether each activity requires mostly muscular strength or muscular endurance. Let's use our signals to answer—thumbs up for muscular strength, thumbs down for muscular endurance, and flat hand if you are not sure. [Point to each illustration and observe student signals. Provide feedback on the responses.] When we were practicing different activities today, we worked on specific muscles.

"What muscles is this activity [point to sit-ups] for? [Ask several similar questions to match exercises with specific muscle groups. Have all children point to the muscles they think are the answers to each question.] When can you practice these activities besides physical education class? Yes, during recess, before and after school, and at home. We'll practice these throughout the year so your muscular strength and endurance should improve."

Look For

- Do the children perform the activities properly? If not, correct the child and watch that the exercise is then done correctly or stop the whole class and review the correct procedure by using a demonstration.

- Can the children correctly describe muscular strength and endurance? Emphasize the distinction that strength is exerting effort for a short period of time and endurance is exerting effort for a long time. Can the children identify the purpose of each activity?

How Can I Change This?

- Add other stations that develop muscular strength and endurance such as arm curls using weighted cans, abdominal curls, pull-ups or chin-ups, sit-ups with a weight, bench stepping, rope or pole climb, and the like.

- In a future lesson, use laminated file cards to help children identify the specific group of muscles different activities exercise. Use five cards (muscular strength, muscular endurance, legs, abdomen, and upper body) for each station. After trying the activity at the station, the children first decide if the exercise is best for improving muscular strength or endurance. Then they decide which part of the body has to work the most to do the activity. One student at the station holds up their cards to show their choices to the whole class. In the beginning, discussions will be necessary to help children think through their choices. You may want to start this learning experience with just identifying the muscle groups (legs, abdomen, or upper body) rather than distinguishing between strength and endurance.

- Provide a scorecard so children can record their scores on the various activities, keep a record of their progress, and try to improve on their performances. See sample muscular strength and endurance scorecard in Figure 8.5.

- Review the meaning of repetitions and sets and have students record the number of sets they do for each exercise on the scorecard.

Name: ___Amanda___   Grade: __4__   Teacher: ___Brand___

Muscular Strength and Endurance

Date

Arm and shoulder	$3/16$	$3/20$							
Bar push-ups	7	10							
Monkey bar climb		2x							
Modified pull-ups	10								
Pull-ups									
Rope climb									
Abdomen									
Sit-ups		15							
Curl-ups									
Crunches	10								
Legs									
Jump the stick	8	6							
Standing long jump									

Figure 8.5 Muscular strength and endurance scorecard.

TEACHABLE MOMENTS

Acknowledge that most activities involve both strength and endurance and determine if an activity should be done only once or twice (strength) or repeated many times (endurance).

Ask students what equipment they could use at home instead of the stations at school? Relate what they use at school to their activities at home.

MUSCLE OF THE MONTH

Objectives

As a result of participating in this learning experience, children will improve their ability to

- identify the major muscle groups in the body
- spell and pronounce major muscle groups, identify what actions they take, and indicate what exercises will make them stronger

Suggested Grade Range

Intermediate (3–6)

Organization

Introduce Muscle of the Month during one class and then revisit the activity for short periods during subsequent classes.

Equipment Needed

Poster featuring the major muscles of the human body

Description

"The major muscles of the human body are shown on this wall poster. Did you know that there are about 600 muscles in the body? During the next month we are going to learn about one of these important muscles. We're going to start with the quadriceps muscle and call this our Muscle of the Month. We'll learn how to spell it, what it does, and what exercises will make it stronger.

"The quadriceps is actually four large muscles in the top part of our leg called the thigh. This muscle group is very strong and helps us do many activities such as kicking, running, jumping, and biking. Today we are going to do a quadriceps activity as part of our warm-up. Because our lesson today will be on kicking and punting, we are going to start by spreading out and pretending to punt a ball. Try this motion and feel your quadriceps muscles when you straighten your leg to kick. Keep practicing your punting motion and feel your quadriceps get tight, then loose. Now do some jumping in place. You can feel your quadriceps muscles working. Now let's do some jumping jacks to finish our warm-up. [Finish your warm-up exercises and call the class in to see the poster or chalkboard.]

"Look at how this muscle name is spelled and say it with me. Quadriceps. *Quad* means four and there are really four separate muscles that make up the quadriceps or thigh muscles. These muscles are very strong and straighten the leg. Next class I'll ask you some questions about the quadriceps muscle and we will do another activity using this muscle."

Look For

- Can children identify the muscle group by saying it, spelling it, showing its location, and showing its function?

How Can I Change This?

- For other quadriceps activities try vertical jumping, the standing long jump, hopping, and kicking a ball.
- Major muscles to include in the Muscle of the Month lessons are biceps, triceps, pectorals, abdominals, hamstrings, trapezius, deltoids, and gastrocnemius. Their functions and some sample activities are listed here:
    - the biceps flex or bend the elbows and arms and allow the body to lift objects, do pull-ups, and climb the playground bars;
    - the triceps extend or straighten the elbows and arms and allow the body to throw, do push-ups, and climb;
    - the pectorals help move the arms to do push-ups, pull-ups, and climb;
    - the abdominals flex the trunk and allow the body to do sit-ups and many gymnastics and dance movements;
    - the hamstrings flex or bend the lower legs and allow the body to run, jump, and leap;
    - the trapezius raises the shoulders for pull-ups;
    - the deltoids move the arms up, forward, and back to allow the body to swim and bat a ball;
    - the gastrocnemius extends the ankles to help the body jump, run, leap, and kick a ball.

Chapter 9

Learning Experiences for Flexibility

The following learning experiences help children practice appropriate stretching exercises and learn the meaning of flexibility, why flexibility is important, and how to use safe stretching to maintain and improve flexibility. Young children benefit by introductory experiences in stretching, whereas older children learn more information about flexibility.

Flexibility exercises are used with many gymnastics, dance, and games lessons. Stretching activities can be used as proper warm-up routines and as ways to improve performance in these motor skills. Reinforce the correct procedures for stretching in all these activities.

Focus	Name	Suggested grade range
Learning to stretch	Stretching Yourself	Pre-K–2
Defining flexibility	Stay Flexed!	3–6
Proper techniques for stretching exercises	Stretch It!	3–6

STRETCHING YOURSELF

Objectives

As a result of participating in this learning experience, children will improve their ability to

- use slow and gentle movements when stretching
- hold the stretched position for 10 counts without bouncing (1-2, #26)
- perform a series of stretches correctly (1-2, #19)

Suggested Grade Range

Primary (Pre-K–2)

Organization

Open area for each student to have a self-space; wall space or easel to display pictures of stretching exercises

Equipment Needed

Illustrations of stretching exercises shown in Figure 9.1 (you can enlarge these pictures and laminate them); clamps, clothespins or tape to hang posters; 1 small mat or carpet square for each student or enough mat space so each child has a self-space

Description

"Today we are going to learn how to stretch. We'll see who is most like the 'rubber-band man'—who stretches very easily. To start I want you to copy my actions. That's right, try to do exactly what I do. You are stretching your arms over your head and reaching for the sky—we'll call this the high-10 stretch. Now bend over and stretch between your legs. This is called hang time! This time sit on the floor and stretch your hands toward your toes. This is called the sit-and-reach. Relax. We should do stretching slowly. Let's try the sit-and-reach again and do it very slowly. Well done! Another thing we should do is hold each stretch for at least 10 counts. Let's try the sit-and-reach again and hold it as we count to 10 together. Ready, stretch and hold, 1, 2, 3, 4, 5, 6, 7, 8, 9, 10, and relax. Let's do one more stretch together. Lie on your back, hug your knees, and point one foot toward the ceiling. Hold it while we count to 10. [Count.] That's great, you were stretching slowly and holding it for 10 counts.

"Now when I give you the signal, I want you to go to the pictures on the wall, choose one and look at it, and then go back to your mat and copy it. Try as many of these as you want, but remember to stretch slowly and count silently to yourself to 10. OK, go. [Watch children and provide feedback to help them do the stretches properly. After about 10 minutes, call the class together for closure.] You've worked on your stretching exercises very well! What makes a good stretch? Yes, Carlos, we must do it slowly. That's right, Michael, we hold it for 10 counts.

"Before you go, show me how to do a stride stretch. [Have all children demonstrate.] Great, you've learned different ways to stretch! We'll practice these all year, so I'll be looking to see who remembers them!"

Figure 9.1 Stretching exercises.

Look For

- Do children stretch gently? If not tell them to show you in slow motion. Do they hold the stretched position for at least 10 counts? Use the counting strategy to remind them. Can they look at the pictures and do the stretches properly? If not, pinpoint students using correct form to demonstrate the correct technique to the class.

How Can I Change This?

- Show each picture one at a time and have the whole class do the stretch together. Plan to give children some time in future classes to look at the pictures and practice the stretches.

> **TEACHABLE MOMENT**
>
> Ask children when they could practice stretching besides in physical education class. Make sure they understand they can stretch at home or during recreational activities.

STAY FLEXED!

Objectives

As a result of participating in this learning experience, children will improve their ability to

- define flexibility as the ability to move joints and the attached muscles through a full range of motion
- perform a variety of stretching exercises by holding the positions for 15 seconds without bouncing
- state the benefits of good flexibility—to help the body to move freely and to reduce the chance of muscle soreness and pain (3-4, #24)

Suggested Grade Range

Intermediate (3–6)

Organization

Basketball court or area with clearly marked lines. Working as partners, students are scattered around the line perimeter. For discussion the class gathers near the sign area.

Equipment Needed

Skeleton or picture model that shows joints (try your science department); large rubber band; colored chalk (at least 2 different colors); posters showing a definition of flexibility, the benefits of good flexibility, and illustrations of stretching exercises (see Figure 9.1); clamps, clothespins or tape to hang posters

Description

"In today's lesson we will learn about the fitness component of flexibility. At the end of the lesson you should be able to answer these questions:

1. What is flexibility?
2. Why is it important to one's health?
3. How do we improve and maintain good flexibility?

"What is flexibility? I hear that it makes us 'able to move our bones,' 'able to bend easily,' and 'you can stretch out.' [Display the poster with the definition of flexibility. Have students read silently, then have someone read aloud.] Flexibility is the ability of the body to move the joints and attached muscles freely through a full range of motion. Everyone needs a healthy level of flexibility so that the body can bend, stretch, and twist freely without hurting.

[Point out the various joints on a skeleton.] "Joints are points where two bones come together. The movement of the joints allows us to move our body. Muscles are attached to the bones and cause the joints to move. [If available, show a model of a joint with connective tissue.] Now I want you to do some movements and feel several joints on your body. Swing your leg back and forth as you do when you kick a ball and feel your knee joint. Now move your hand and arm up and down like a biceps curl and feel your elbow joint. Swing your leg back and forth and feel your hip joint. Bend your ankle up and down and feel the ankle joint. All these joints are bones with muscle and connective tissue surrounding them.

"Now we're going to use a rubber band to represent the muscle so you can watch the stretching action. I'll need one of you to demonstrate flexibility. OK, Evan, hold this large rubber band at the base of your lower back. Now I'm going to pull the band down to the back of your knee. Now bend over and touch your knees. Now bend further and reach for your toes. The rubber band shows how your muscle stretches.

"Now you can all do a flexibility experiment. You will work as partners and measure each others' performance on a modified sit-and-reach task. One of you will sit on the floor with your legs slightly apart and fully extended. Flex your heels and keep them on a line. Lean forward at the hip, reach as far as you can, and hold for 3 counts. The other partner should mark with chalk the distance your fingertips reach. Repeat this for the other partner using a different color chalk.

"Now one of you will be the exerciser and the other the nonexerciser. The nonexerciser will lie on the floor and relax while the exerciser will perform a series of exercises. I want you to do the crossover hang; the sit-and-reach; straddle right, left, and center; and hang time. [Show the poster of stretching exercises.] For each exercise stretch slow and steady for 15 counts. Don't bounce. [Allow 3 to 5 minutes for stretching.] OK, exercisers, well done! Now repeat the sit-and-reach task and mark the distance reached by the exerciser and nonexerciser. Which person was able to improve the stretch and reach farther the second time? You're all saying that the exerciser improved. Why? That's right, the stretching exercises warmed up the joint and muscles so they moved more easily. How could this information help a person who is playing sports or participating in physical activities? Yes, it can help them move more freely and keep them from getting hurt. So, let's review the benefits of good flexibility. Flexibility can help the body to move freely; it lets the body bend, stretch, and twist through a bigger range of motion; and it reduces the chances of muscle soreness and pain if you do it regularly. We'll be practicing and testing our flexibility throughout the year to see if your muscles stretch easily!"

Look For

- Can students describe flexibility? Can they state some benefits? Do they stretch gently and hold the stretches for 15 or more counts?

How Can I Change This?

- If you have gymnastics benches or bleacher benches, students can put their feet against the base of the bench and stretch at shoulder level to the top of the bench. This would be similar to the standard fitness sit-and-reach test, so students could periodically test themselves.
- To simplify flexibility for the primary grades, show them the skeleton and explain that flexibility lets the body bend, stretch, and twist freely without hurting the joints or muscles. Demonstrate and have children practice the slow counting for holding stretches.
- Select several flexibility tasks to self-test the flexibility of the shoulders, trunk, hips, and legs. Organize a circuit or have students work as partners. See Corbin and Lindsey (1990) and Foster, Hartinger, and Smith (1992) in the suggested readings for excellent examples.

TEACHABLE MOMENTS

Discuss the idea of "use it or lose it." The benefits of doing stretching exercises are short-lived unless a person continues to stretch on a regular basis. You can mention the FIT principle here.

Explain that lower back pain is a very frequent adult problem. Some adults complain about their "aching backs." Eight of 10 adults have problems with their back. Many do not exercise regularly so they become weaker and less flexible and their muscles are easily strained and sore. That's why students should develop the habit of regular physical activity and stretch daily.

(4)

STRETCH IT!

Objectives

As a result of participating in this learning experience, children will improve their ability to

- demonstrate proper technique for doing a series of stretching exercises (5-6, #15)
- understand that flexibility is maintained only by doing stretching exercises on a regular basis (5-6, #18)

Suggested Grade Range

Intermediate (3–6)

Organization

Wall space for a poster display and room for children to stretch (see Figure 9.2)

Equipment Needed

Posters illustrating each stretching exercise (see Figure 9.1) and containing information on correct stretching procedures (should be slow and gentle, held for 15 or more counts, no bouncing, knees soft, and done daily), 1 carpet square for each student, music (like "Movin'" by Hap Palmer, and "Disco Dances and Games" by Jill Galina, both from Kimbo Educational Records—see Additional Resources) and player

Description

"In a previous lesson we learned the definition of the fitness component called *flexibility*. Turn to your neighbor and tell him or her what flexibility means. Did your neighbor mention both joints and muscles? Did that person say something about moving through a full range of motion? [Show the definition poster and review.] When I say 'signal

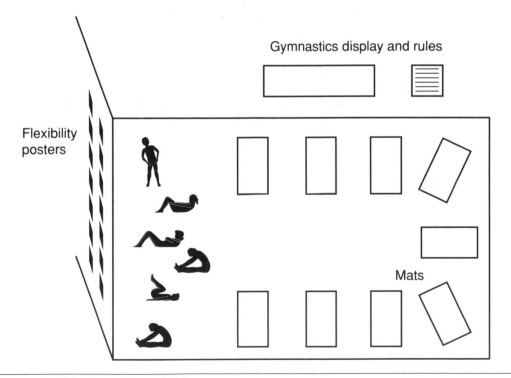

Figure 9.2 Diagram of Stretch It!

now' show me a thumbs up signal if you think you should bounce as you stretch. Use a thumbs down signal if you think that you shouldn't bounce. Show a flat hand if you are unsure. OK, signal now. [Afterward] This time tell your neighbor how long to hold the stretch. Thumbs up if you say less than 10; thumbs down if you say 15. That's right, 15. Using your fingers to signal, how many times a week should stretching be done? Good! I see four, five, and six. Remember, you should stretch at least three times a week, but daily is best. Can you name some sports or activities that require a high level of flexibility? I'm hearing dance, gymnastics, track and field events—all of those are good answers and there are many others.

[Point out the poster stretches.] "What are these pictures showing? Yes, Travis, they are different ways and parts of the body to stretch. These posters are to help you practice stretching as part of your warm-up for gymnastics. On the signal jog around the lesson area while the music is playing. When the music stops, come to your space in front of the flexibility display. [Have students jog 2 or 3 minutes.] Today we will take time to review the stretching exercises, but next time you can do them on your own. [Demonstrate each stretch from Figure 9.1.] Practice with me and count silently while I keep time for 15 seconds. [This will help students develop a better sense of how long 15 seconds really is.]

"The next time you come to physical education class, I'd like you to automatically begin warming up by jogging to the music. Then come to the poster display and start doing the stretching exercises. This will make your muscles ready to move and stretch far."

Look For

- Are children using the correct form? If not, stop and review so they don't develop bad habits. Many children will not hold the stretch for 15 or more seconds. You will have to continually work on this and positively reinforce those children who are stretching correctly.

How Can I Change This?

- Choose several warm-up leaders. The posters are helpful to show them what to do.
- Ask students to select any six stretches from the display and use them to warm up before beginning the gymnastics work.
- Ask students to draw pictures of stretching exercises that are not on the posters. Add them to the list.
- Use an aerobic dance routine for warm-up instead of jogging or have students practice locomotor movements and step-like movements in a scattered formation.

TEACHABLE MOMENTS

When showing the proper position for a specific stretch discuss harmful positions. See chapter 4 for examples.

If students participate in karate, gymnastics, dance, or similar activities have them explain why they need a high level of flexibility to do the activity.

Ask students to compare stretching before and after doing gymnastics. Did they find it easier or harder to stretch? Why? (Stretching after the muscles are warm from a whole-body activity is best.)

Discuss the principle of specificity. In order to increase the flexibility of a particular body part, the joints and muscles in that area must be stretched regularly. Leg stretches won't help shoulder flexibility!

Chapter 10

Learning Experiences for Healthy Habits and Wellness

This chapter presents learning experiences that teach children ways to keep the body healthy and performing at optimum efficiency. Learning experiences in this category are intended to supplement, not take the place of, regular classroom instruction on topics of health and nutrition. The purposes are to reinforce positive health habits the children learn in their regular classroom lessons and to link these concepts with the benefits of regular physical activity.

Excellent learning experiences for developing healthy habits are available through the American Cancer Society, the American Heart Association, and private companies like the McDonald's Educational Resources Center and Slim Goodbody Video-Kits. Many of the materials are free or have only a nominal cost (see Additional Resources). The learning experiences in this chapter are examples of how healthy habits and wellness concepts can be taught in a physical education setting.

Focus	Name	Suggested grade range
Meaning of a calorie	Cookie Lesson	3–6
Setting personal fitness goals	Goal Setting	3–6

COOKIE LESSON

Objectives

As a result of participating in this learning experience, children will improve their ability to

- explain the meaning of a calorie
- explain the meaning of caloric balance and give examples of intake and output

Suggested Grade Range

Intermediate (3–6)

Organization

Outside or inside area suitable for whole class dribbling activities

Equipment Needed

Poster or chalkboard; 1 cookie for each student; 8-1/2-inch playground balls (1 per child); several boxes to spread out and hold balls; lively music ("Sneaky Snake" from *Fun Activities for Perceptual Motor Skills*, Kimbo Educational records—see Additional Resources for ordering information)

Description

"We have a different way to start class today that I think you'll like! Please sit in a circle while I pass around the bag of cookies. Each person please take only one cookie.

"In today's lesson we will be learning about calories. Each cookie has approximately 60 calories. A calorie is a way to measure energy; just like a ruler can measure inches. [Show the word *calorie* with the definition on chalkboard or poster.] I would like you to eat the cookie before we start our activities. [The skill theme focus of this lesson can vary, but it must be filled with continuous activity—like dribbling.]

"We are going to review our dribbling skills and play some dribbling games today, while keeping our calories in mind. Select a ball from the box, find your self-space, and begin to dribble your ball by alternating hands and dribbling around your feet. [Continue for about 2 minutes, adding other challenges like turning while dribbling and alternating hands.]

"Now I want you to dribble and travel around the general space inside the boundaries. Listen closely for the stop signal and control your ball so you avoid others. Go! [Continue for about 4 minutes, adding challenges like changing direction, pathway, and speed.]

[Signal stop.] "Now let's play Stop and Go using music. When the music is playing dribble and travel quickly. When the music stops see how quickly you can stop and hold the ball. [Let children travel for 10 to 20 seconds and give them the stop signal; then vary the stop and go time intervals to challenge their control. Continue for 3 to 5 minutes.]

"This time when the music plays, practice accelerating and decelerating. That's right—gradually speed up and go fast, and then slow down. Try changing from fast to slow and back to fast several times. Remember, when the music stops, then you stop. Ready, go. [Continue the activity for several minutes, observing for clear changes in speed. Use pinpointing to refine if needed.] Because you are experienced dribblers let's play Protect the Ball with partners. Sit down next to a person near you and watch the demonstration of Protect the Ball. One partner will dribble in personal space and use skills for protecting the ball. That's right, keep your body between the ball and your opponent and switch hands. The other partner tries to steal the ball or cause the dribbler to lose control. You'll play for 1 minute with the same dribbler continuing to practice. The defender must return the ball if stolen or knocked away. Spread out and decide who will be the first dribbler. [Check to see that children are spread out and then start. After 1 minute, have the children trade roles.]

"Everyone stop and listen to the new directions. Now you have a choice. You can continue to take turns with one dribbler and one defender and decide how long to practice. Or you can play Steal It If You Can. This means that if the defender steals the ball then that person immediately becomes the dribbler. You and your partner start to play as soon as you decide.

[After the 20-minute lesson, call students in to the circle for a discussion of calories.] "Remember the cookie I gave to you in the beginning of the lesson? How many calories did it contain? That's right, 60 calories. So you had 60 units of energy to start the lesson. During today's lesson we worked on basketball skills and you—your muscles— were using energy, so you were using up calories. Playing basketball uses about 3 calories per minute. You worked for 20 minutes, so what math operation can we use to find out how many total calories we used up doing the lesson? That's right, multiplication. So we multiply 20 times 3 and get 60 calories. Calories that you use up in activity are called output and calories that you eat or take in are called input. If they are equal then we have a caloric balance. [Show the caloric balance equation on the poster or chalkboard.] I gave you 60 calories in the beginning of the lesson, and you used up 60 calories by exercising, so we are even! We'll talk more about caloric input and output during the year, and what happens when your balance *isn't* even."

Look For

- Do students understand the meaning of a calorie? Do they understand the caloric balance equation?

How Can I Change This?

- Use other activities to provide an active lesson.
- Use tables of caloric values for foods and activities to practice recording the caloric value for common foods and the caloric value for physical activities.
- Have students take the day's lunch menu and record the calories it contains. Then have them write down all the activities they will engage in from lunch to supper and figure out the total calories the activities will use. Compare the total calories for food intake and activity output to see if the result is an excess, deficit, or equal number.

TEACHABLE MOMENT

Discuss how many calories are used when watching television. Discuss how many calories are equal to 1 pound (3,500 calories). What is necessary to maintain a steady body weight?

GOAL SETTING

Objectives

As a result of participating in this learning experience, children will improve their ability to

- use the healthy standard scores on a health-related fitness test to relate to their personal level of fitness
- set personal goals for improvement or maintenance of fitness levels for the health-related components (5-6, #18)
- design strategies with the help of the teacher to help them achieve personal fitness goals successfully

Suggested Grade Range

Intermediate (3–6)

Organization

A classroom or space suitable for writing

Equipment Needed

1 completed Physical Best fitness report card for each student (see Figure 10.1); 1 copy for every 2 students of the Physical Best Health-Related Fitness Standards (contact AAHPERD at 1900 Association Drive, Reston, VA 22091-1599 or 1-800-321-0789); 1 poster of suggested goals for the fitness components and test items (see Figure 10.2).

Description

"Now that you have completed all the fitness tests we can look at the results and set some goals for you to shoot for. First, let's review the purpose of the physical fitness tests—they give you information on your present fitness level for different fitness components. You can use this information to plan how to improve the fitness areas you're weak in and maintain healthy or high scores. [Hand out the Physical Best report cards.]

"Now that everyone has their own scores, follow along as I explain the format. Column 1 shows the fitness component, column 2 the type of test, and column 3 your present score for each item. Later in this lesson you will write in your goals for maintaining or improving your personal fitness. Later in the year, you will do a final evaluation to measure your progress in reaching your fitness goals.

"Look at column 3, your score, and compare it with the health fitness standards that I am handing out. [It helps to also have a large chart or poster of the standards to refer to during the lesson.] Locate your age and read the results across from the first fitness component, aerobic endurance. For example, the standard for a 9-year-old boy in the 1-mile run is 10 minutes; for a 9-year-old girl it is 11 minutes. Now look at your results for the mile. If you met the standard or if your score was even lower than the standard, for example 9 minutes, then your aerobic endurance is at a healthy level. You want to write the word *maintain*, which means that you will continue to do exercises and play games and sports that will keep your heart and lungs strong and healthy. If you had a higher score than the standard, then choose from one of the suggested goals listed on the goal-setting poster [see Figure 10.2].

"If your score was close to the healthy standard, a reduction of 30 seconds or 1 minute may be your best choice. If you have a higher score for the mile run, say 18 to 20

REPORT CARD

_____
Name

_____
Age

_____
Grade

Fitness component	Test Item		Score Date _____	My goal	Score after training Date _____
Aerobic endurance	Distance run (check one) Mile _____ 1/2 Mile _____ Other _____				
Body composition	Skin folds (check those used)	1. Subscapular			
		2. Triceps			
		3. Calf			
		Sum of 2 & 3			
	OR BMI				
Flexibility	Sit and reach				
Abdominal strength/endurance	Sit-ups				
Upper body strength/endurance	(check one) Pull-ups _____ **OR** Modified pull-ups _____				

Figure 10.1   Physical Best report card. *Note.* Reprinted by permission of American Alliance for Health, Physical Education, Recreation and Dance, 1988.

If you met or did better than the healthy standard, you can write maintain *for your goal. If you did not achieve the healthy standard choose one of the suggested goals for each component.*

Test item	Suggested goal
Mile	30 seconds less 1 minute less 1-1/2 minutes less 2 minutes less 3 minutes less
Sit-and-reach	1 centimeter more 2 centimeters more
Sit-ups	5 more 10 more
Pull-ups	1 more
Modified pull-ups	3 more 5 more
Flexed-arm hang	3 seconds more 5 seconds more

Figure 10.2   Suggested fitness goals.

minutes, you may be able to reduce your score by 2 to 3 minutes. Now you decide on your goal for just the aerobic endurance component and I'll come around to help you if you need it. [Circulate to help individuals write down their goals.]

"In the mile run, the lower your time the better your level of aerobic fitness is. But for the remaining items, the higher your score the better your fitness level. [Because of the impact of factors such as heredity and home influences on food choices and intake we do not have children set goals for body composition. Comprehensive intervention programs involving the parents are recommended for obese children.]

"Now let's look at your sit-and-reach scores. A healthy score is 25 centimeters. If your score is 25 or more, you can write *maintain*. If you want to try to improve, write only 1 centimeter because you are already at a high level. If your score was lower than 25, choose 1 or 2 centimeters, depending on how often you plan to work on stretching. Now follow the same procedure for sit-ups. Compare your score with the standard and select a reasonable goal by looking at the goal-setting poster. I'll come by and check your goals if you want help. Now for upper body muscular strength and endurance. We tried several different tasks, so check your scores for those tasks and compare them to the standards. Choose your goals and write them in. [Collect the report cards, review their goals, and make comments or suggestions as needed. Return the cards in a future class when you are working on fitness activities so that students can continue to work toward their personal goals.] Now that you have set your goals, let's talk about how to achieve them. What are some strategies we can use to reach our goals? We can use a variety of activities so we don't get bored from doing the same thing all the time. Remember the FIT principle? We can increase the frequency, intensity, and time of our activities. We can do the activities regularly—every day if possible, and at least three times a week. We can gradually increase the level or intensity of work. Maybe we'll start with 15 sit-ups. Then we'll do two sets of 15 and later we'll do three sets of 15. We might start with jogging 3 to 5 minutes, then increase to 8 minutes, and then 10 minutes. You'll have to exercise outside of physical education class to meet your goals. You can practice your fitness activities at recess and at home. At recess have fun climbing the bars, practice pull-ups, play tag, or jump rope. At home play soccer with friends, ride bikes, skate, or take a walk. Ask your parents to count how many sit-ups or push-ups you can do in 1 minute. Practice stretching while watching TV.

Keep a record of your workouts. List the activities you do on a calendar or write down your exercises in a diary. Be positive and try your best at physical activities even when you don't enjoy everything we do. For example, some of you love to play soccer; others prefer basketball. Some of you like to run; others prefer to walk. No matter what the physical education lesson or activity, have a positive attitude. At different times throughout the year, we'll have activities that are your favorites.

"Remember the slogan 'use it or lose it.' You'll want to maintain your healthy fitness levels and work harder on weaker components. Remember that more improvement is possible in a weak area than a healthy one.

"A person's physical fitness is not static or set. It is continually changing and evolving due to your continued growth and development. Choosing to be active on a regular basis and to include all the components of physical fitness in your exercise routine is the best way to achieve a healthy level of fitness. This will not happen overnight. It takes time and real effort to stay in good shape! I'll give you opportunities to check your progress on these fitness components during the next few months."

Look For

- Make sure children understand how to interpret their own scores and how to compare their scores with the health standards. To check for understanding ask such questions as "What would the healthy standard be for a 12-year-old girl in the mile run?"

- Look at sample report cards to see if students understand how to set appropriate goals. Help children adjust their goals to ensure that they can improve with reasonable effort—it's better to set goals that are too easy than too hard. Can children name some strategies for accomplishing their goals?

How Can I Change This?

- You may want to modify the standards to suit your students and provide the opportunity for success for all children. For a few children, running a mile is too difficult, so arrange for them to run a half mile in the initial evaluation. Then their goal can be to run three-quarters of a mile and eventually a full mile.

- Test one component at a time. Set goals and strategies for the sit-up test and then do activities related to that component. Follow up with feedback on students' efforts and learn the procedures for goal setting. Then you can concentrate on another component and eventually cover all of them.

- Have children write out their goals and the activities they plan to engage in to reach them. This can take the form of a contract and parents can verify when activities are accomplished.

TEACHABLE MOMENTS

Help children learn that maintaining healthy fitness levels requires regular, consistent, lifetime activity. Physical fitness should be a lifelong habit.

Some children will tend to set unreasonable goals. Explain that most people can't attain large improvements in just a few days. It takes consistent practice for many days and weeks to achieve small improvements. It is important that children enjoy the good feelings and benefits that accrue each time they exercise.

So Where Do We Go From Here?

We hope that reading this book has left you full of thoughts, some questions, and most of all, *excitement* about teaching this content area. We hope it makes you eager to get out there and try some of the ideas and learning experiences with your children . . . to take a closer look at your curriculum . . . to maybe give you that "something extra" you needed in order to take another try at teaching this content to your children.

And although we know that implementing many of the ideas in this book with your children probably won't be quite as easy as it was to read about them, we hope that this book goes a long way in helping you to get there. We hope that it encourages you to talk with other teachers, ask questions, and search for solutions that will make your teaching, and your students' learning experiences, the best they can be!

We here in the Child Health Division of Human Kinetics want you to know that you're not out there alone in your quest to improve your teaching and the physical education experiences of your students. We do our best to provide you with current information and professional support through our many programs and resources. Examples of these include our American Master Teacher Program for Children's Physical Education (AMTP), which this book is a part of; the national newsletter *Teaching Elementary Physical Education (TEPE)*; the annual national Conference on Teaching Elementary Physical Education, which we cosponsor, and our outcomes-based student and teacher resources.

Many of you have written or called us in the past with a neat idea you wanted to share with others in *TEPE*, a question on where to find some information, or even just to say thanks for a job well done. We hope that you'll continue to let us know what your questions, concerns, and thoughts are and how we can help you even better in the future. Feel free to write us at P.O. Box 5076, Champaign, IL 61825-5076, or call us at 1-800-747-4457. We'll do our best to help you out!

Until then,

The staff of the Child Health Division
of Human Kinetics

References

American Alliance for Health, Physical Education, Recreation and Dance. (1980). *Health related fitness test*. Reston, VA: Author.

American Alliance for Health, Physical Education, Recreation and Dance. (1989). *Physical best*. Reston, VA: Author.

Belka, D. (1994). *Teaching children games: Becoming a master teacher*. Champaign, IL: Human Kinetics.

Blair, S.N., Kohl, H.W., Paffenbarger, R.S., Clarke, D.G., Cooper, K.H., & Gibbons, L.W. (1989). Physical fitness and all-cause mortality: A prospective study of healthy men and women. *Journal of the American Medical Association*, **262**, 2395-2401.

Buschner, C. (1994). *Teaching children movement concepts and skills: Becoming a master teacher*. Champaign, IL: Human Kinetics.

Corbin, C.B. (1987). Physical fitness in the K-12 curriculum: Some defensible solutions to perennial problems. *Journal of Physical Education, Recreation and Dance*, **58**(7), 49-54.

Corbin, C.B., & Lindsey, R. (1991). *Concepts of physical fitness with laboratories* (7th ed.). Dubuque, IA: Brown.

Council on Physical Education for Children. (1992). *Developmentally appropriate physical education practices for children*. Reston, VA: National Association for Sport and Physical Education.

Franck, M., Graham, G., Lawson, H., Loughrey, T., Ritson, R., Sanborn, M., & Seefeldt, V. (1991). *Physical education outcomes: A project of the National Association for Sport and Physical Education*. Reston, VA: National Association for Sport and Physical Education.

Gilliam, T.B., MacConnie, S.E., Geenen, D.L., Pels, A.E., & Freedson, P.S. (1982). Exercise programs for children: A way to prevent heart disease? *Physician and Sportsmedicine*, **10**(9), 96-109.

Graham, G. (1992). *Teaching children physical education: Becoming a master teacher*. Champaign, IL: Human Kinetics.

Kelly, L.E. (1989). Instructional time: The overlooked factor in PE curriculum development. *Journal of Physical Education, Recreation and Dance*, **60**(6), 29-32.

Kraus, H., & Hirschland, R.P. (1954). Minimum muscular fitness tests in school children. *Research Quarterly*, **25**, 178-188.

Pate, R.R. (1983). A new definition of youth fitness. *Physician and Sportsmedicine*, **11**(4), 77-83.

Purcell, T. (1994). *Teaching children dance: Becoming a master teacher*. Champaign, IL: Human Kinetics.

Ross, J.G, & Gilbert, G.G. (1985). The national children and youth fitness study: A summary of findings. *Journal of Physical Education, Recreation and Dance*, **56**(1), 45-50.

Ross, J.G, & Pate, R.R. (1987). The national children and youth fitness study II: A summary of findings. *Journal of Physical Education, Recreation and Dance*, **58**(9), 51-56.

Rowland, T.W. (1990). *Exercise and children's health*. Champaign, IL: Human Kinetics.

Sander, A.N., & Burton, E.C. (1989). Learning aids—Enhancing fitness knowledge in elementary physical education. *Journal of Physical Education, Recreation and Dance*, **60**(1), 56-59.

Seefeldt, V. (1986). *Physical activity and well-being*. Reston, VA: American Alliance for Health, Physical Education, Recreation and Dance.

Siedentop, D. (1991). *Developing teaching skills in physical education* (3rd ed.). Palo Alto, CA: Mayfield.

Simons-Morton, B.G., O'Hara, N.M., Simons-Morton, D.G., & Parcel, G.S. (1987). Children and fitness: A public health perspective. *Research Quarterly for Exercise and Sport*, **58**(4), 295-302.

Werner, P. (1994). *Teaching children gymnastics: Becoming a master teacher*. Champaign, IL: Human Kinetics.

Suggested Readings

Cooper, K. (1991). *Kid fitness*. New York: Bantam.

A book for parents, teachers, and coaches on exercise and nutrition for children and adolescents. Includes information about child development, motivational strategies, exercise programs, and nutritional advice to promote children's physical fitness and self-esteem.

Corbin, C.B. (1987). Physical fitness in the K-12 curriculum: Some defensible solutions to perennial problems. *Journal of Physical Education, Recreation and Dance*, **58**(7), 49-54.

Outlines the important outcomes of a physical fitness curriculum. Explains the importance of helping students learn fitness information to become knowledgeable fitness consumers. Describes problems associated with teaching fitness in schools and offers constructive solutions.

Corbin, C.B., & Lindsey, R. (1990). *Fitness for life* (3rd ed.). Glenview, IL: Scott, Foresman.

Textbook for junior high and high school students, though some experiences can be adapted for children. Includes self-evaluation activities, worksheets to record results, and test questions.

Corbin, C.B., & Lindsey, R. (1991). *Concepts of physical fitness with laboratories* (7th ed.). Dubuque, IA: Brown.

Textbook designed for an introductory college-level physical fitness and exercise class. Excellent detailed fitness information.

Corbin, C.B., & Pangrazi, R.P. (1989). *Teaching strategies for improving youth fitness*. Dallas: Institute for Aerobics Research.

Fitness information and learning activities for elementary through high school students.

Foster, E.R., Hartinger, K., & Smith, K.A. (1992). *Fitness fun*. Champaign, IL: Human Kinetics.

A variety of field-tested activities to help children develop cardiorespiratory fitness, muscular strength, muscular endurance, and flexibility.

Human Kinetics. (in press). *Teaching for outcomes in elementary physical education: A guide for curriculum and assessment*. Champaign, IL: Human Kinetics.

This unique resource is divided into two parts. Part I introduces the concept of purposeful planning (creating curriculum goals or outcomes that are realistic and achievable for your particular situation) and then shows how to assess these goals using portfolio and performance task assessments. Teachers will find the many practical hints helpful, especially concerning the use and scoring of these assessments. Part II is organized according to the concepts (including fitness concepts) and skills taught in physical education and provides sample performance and portfolio tasks; teachers can use many of these to directly assess NASPE "Benchmarks," which are referenced when applicable. The "learnable pieces" are detailed for each skill and concept, along with activity ideas and practical hints for teaching them at the varying grade levels.

McSwegin, P.J. (Ed.) (1989). *Journal of Physical Education, Recreation and Dance*, **60**(1), 30-45.

A special feature with several articles on planning a fitness curriculum, fitness testing, helping students set goals, and keeping students motivated.

Petray, C.K., & Blazer, S.L. (1991). *Health related physical fitness: Concepts and activities for elementary school children* (3rd ed.). Edina, MN: Bellwether Press/A Division of Burgess International Group.

Textbook written for teachers includes comprehensive information about health-related fitness with practical activities for children.

Rowland, T.W. (1990). *Exercise and children's health*. Champaign, IL: Human Kinetics.

Comprehesive reference book describes the changes in physiological responses to exercise that occur as children grow, summarizes the evidence linking exercise to health in children, and provides guidelines for helping children develop more active lifestyles.

Simons-Morton, B.G., O'Hara, N.M., Simons-Morton, D.G., & Parcel, G.S. (1987). Children and fitness: A public health perspective. *Research Quarterly for Exercise and Sport*, **58**(4), 295-302.

Summarizes the following issues regarding children's physical fitness: current status of children's cardiorespiratory fitness; effects of childhood training programs on the fitness of children and adults; extent of children's participation in moderate to vigorous physical activity; and potential for and the role of physical education in promoting children's lifelong fitness and health.

Whitehead, J.R. (1992). A selected, annotated bibliography for fitness educators. *Journal of Physical Education, Recreation and Dance*, **63**(5), 53-64.

A comprehensive annotated bibliography on the topic of youth fitness that provides excellent references for fitness educators.

Williams, C.S., Harageones, E.G., Johnson, D.J., & Smith, C.D. (1986). *Personal fitness: Looking good/feeling good*. Dubuque, IA: Kendall/Hunt.

A comprehensive fitness program designed for a high school physical fitness course. Includes a textbook and activity handbook for the student and a videotape and resource guide for the teacher.

Additional Resources

American Cancer Society (listed in white pages of the telephone book)

Instructional package for teachers containing lesson plans and videotapes related to student wellness.

American Heart Association (listed in white pages of the telephone book)

Program Packages: Contain teacher's guide, posters, videotapes, and learning experiences related to cardiorespiratory fitness and wellness, including "The Heart Treasure Chest" (for students ages 3 to 5 years) and "Getting to Know Your Heart" (curriculum materials for lower and upper elementary).

Fit to Achieve Elementary Cardiovascular Education Program
University of North Florida
Physical Education Program
Division of Curriculum & Instruction
University of North Florida
4567 St. Johns Bluff Rd.
Jacksonville, FL 32224

Cardiovascular educational fitness materials include two instructional videos, student assignments and worksheets, a teacher's guide, and a parent's guide. For two 13-minute videotape programs and printed materials, send a check for $20 payable to Division of Curriculum and Instruction.

Fitness Walking Materials
Creative Walking Incorporated
P.O. Box 50296
Clayton, MO 63105

Information to help you design a walking wellness curriculum for children. A workbook for elementary students, a teacher's guide of lesson ideas, a newsletter, and motivational materials are available to help teach fitness activities to children.

Healthy Growing Up
McDonald's Education Resource Center
P.O. Box 8002
St. Charles, IL 60174-8002
1-800-627-7646

Lessons to encourage children (Grades K–3) to adopt lifelong habits of good nutrition, exercise, and self-esteem.

Kimbo Educational Records
P.O. Box 477
Long Branch, NJ 07740-0477
1-800-631-2187

Aerobic exercise videotapes for children.

Slim Goodbody Presents All Fit
Human Kinetics
P.O. Box 5076
Champaign, IL 61825-5076

This video program features 15 15-minute lessons that contain vigorous, structured exercises easily done in the classroom, each highlighting a fitness topic and a major muscle group.

The companion *Teacher's Guide* contains lesson plans with pre- and post-viewing activities, ideas on how to integrate fitness concepts into other parts of a curriculum, and reproducible activity sheets to reinforce fitness concepts and challenge students.

Slim Goodbody VideoKits
AV Instructional Services
Agency for Instructional Technology
Box A
Bloomington, IN 47402-9973

"The Inside Story": Ten 15-minute video programs present the exciting story of the human body, with working models of organs and body systems.

"Well, Well, Well": This series of fifteen 15-minute video programs shows how even young children can take an active part in protecting and maintaining their good health. The emphasis is on wellness, safety, nutrition, exercise, and handling feelings in a healthy way.

About the Authors

Tom and Laraine Ratliffe became interested in teaching fitness concepts during the mid-1970s while working as laboratory assistants for Dr. Russell Pate, a nationally recognized authority on children's fitness. Since then they have been actively involved in passing on the message that fitness is important for children through numerous presentations and workshops at the international, national, state, and local levels. They also have published many articles in the *Journal of Physical Education, Recreation and Dance*, the *Journal of Teaching in Physical Education*, and *The Physical Educator*.

Tom Ratliffe is an assistant professor of physical education at The Florida State University. He received his EdD in physical education teacher education from the University of Georgia in 1984. Tom's extensive academic background has given him excellent experience in curriculum design, motor development, teaching methods, and student assessment. For 7 years he was an elementary physical educator who taught fitness concepts and promoted children's fitness. He taught physical education teacher preparation courses at the University of Georgia and the University of Massachusetts at

Amherst. He was also involved in the "Goodbodies" after-school health and fitness program for overweight children.

Tom is a member of the American Alliance for Health, Physical Education, Recreation and Dance, the American Educational Research Association, and the Florida Alliance for Health, Physical Education, Recreation and Dance (FAHPERD).

Laraine McCravey Ratliffe is a physical educator for Grades K-3 at the Florida State University School. Since 1972 her role as a teacher has given her valuable hands-on experience in developing and refining fitness curriculum materials for children. Her involvement also extends outside of the classroom—whether teaching in the "Goodbodies" program or organizing fitness clubs at elementary schools, she is committed to helping children learn about and experience the benefits and joy of regular physical activity.

Laraine received her undergraduate degree from Appalachian State University and her MAT in physical education teacher education in 1976 from the University of South Carolina.